SNORKELLING
IN THE
RED SEA

SWAN·HILL
PRESS

A

SNORKELLING
IN THE
RED SEA

Text and photographs
Claudio Cangini
Nadia Alzani

Translation
Studio Traduzioni
Vecchia, Milan

Maps
Maurizio Dondi

Graphic Design
Clara Zanotti

Drawings
Claudio Nazzaro

CONTENTS

B

1 — The waters of the Red Sea are home to about a thousand different species of fish, about a hundred of which are endemic. The photo shows a Pterois volitans swimming elegantly over a large gorgonian.

2,3 — Three batfish (Platax teira) illuminate the seabed with silvery flashes.

A — Corals from Egyptian seabeds come in various forms, soft and flexible or similar to rocks.

B — The wall of the reef facing the open sea has the greatest abundance of life.

First Published in the UK in 2000
by Swan Hill Press, an imprint of Airlife Publishing Ltd.

British Library Cataloguing-in-Publication Data
A catalogue record for this book
is available from the British Library

ISBN 1 84037 224 9

Printed in Italy

SWAN HILL PRESS
an imprint of Airlife Publishing Ltd.
101 Longden Road, Shrewsbury SY3 9EB, England
E-mail: airlife@airlifebooks.com
Website: www.airlifebooks.com

EGYPT

SINAI

GULF OF SUEZ

STRAIT OF GOBAL

Nuweiba

Monastery of St. Catherine

Dahab

El-Tur

Naama Bay

Sharm el-Sheikh

1-2-3-4

TAWILA ISLAND

*—12

13-14
15-16

9

*

5-6

SHADWAN ISLAND

7-8

Ras Mohammed

TIRAN ISLAND

Hurghada

GIFTUN ISLAND

SANAFIR ISLAND

20-21-22-23

10-11

17-18-19

RED SEA

INTRODUCTION

Snorkeling is an easy, safe and pleasant activity that people of any age can enjoy. It requires no special physical skills or abilities: an ideal sport for the whole family!

Through snorkeling, anyone can explore the underwater world without the need for heavy equipment or special certifications. By simply putting on a mask, a snorkel, and a pair of flippers and immersing your face just under the surface of the sea, you can open a window to a marvelous world that will give you unforgettable thrills.

The coast of the Egyptian Red Sea offers unique, fascinating sights, and the coral reef is without doubt the most interesting environment of this coastal ecosystem. It's exciting to discover the reef and its extraordinary inhabitants, like taking a fantastic voyage to a magical, unreal world. As you see a succession of bizarre shapes, explosions of color and a myriad of fish, you'll immediately understand the complexity of the coral structures and the creatures swimming around them. It's a world that existed millions of years before we appeared on the Earth, an environment governed by

rise from the depths to the surface, where the waves crash against them. The Red Sea is a tropical sea that's pleasant for diving, as the temperature never descends lower than 20°C. This characteristic, along with the water's high salinity (about 40%) has helped create a biological environment of incomparable beauty. It's practically a closed sea, as the underwater shelf that connects it to the Indian Ocean, the Bab el-Mandeb sill, is only 100 meters deep. The absence of tributary rivers except for

fragile balances, a world we must approach with extreme respect, careful to cause absolutely no harm. We're guests in someone else's home and we need to mind our manners! As the plane flies in for a landing near the Red Sea, you'll see a breathtaking spectacle from the window: intricate banks of stony corals rising to the surface wind along the coast, forming lagoons and shallow waters where the color of the sea runs from delicate azure to bright emerald to the intense blue of the abyss. The coral agglomerates can vary greatly in form and size. Some cover less than a square meter, while others continue uninterrupted for dozens of miles.

These walls built by tiny animals

A – Even sandy and detrital seabeds are full of life. The photograph shows a stingray mimetizing in the sand.

B – Soft corals like Alcyonaria are the most colorful. Where biological conditions are optimal, these Octocorals develop in an extraordinary manner.

C – The coastal reef of the Red Sea appears as a belt of corals parallel to the coast surrounding a shallow lagoon on the mainland side.

D – The variety of colors and forms of life on the coral reef appears as

soon as you immerse your head beneath the water's surface. Numberless glassfish and sponges integrate each other according to a delicate equilibrium.

E – The sandy seabeds contain stony coral pinnacles rising toward the surface. Just a few meters contains countless layers of organisms like stony coral, sponges and alcyonarians

F – Various evolutionary phases have led each inhabitant of the reef to occupy its own special position. The photograph shows a gorgonian and an alcyonarian that compete to obtain vital room.

A

B

B – Red Sea fish have bright, gaudy colors. The yellowband angelfish (Pomacanthus maculosus) is one of the more showy examples.

C – The boxfish (Ostracion cubicus) is one of the strangest inhabitants of the reef. Its square form and sturdy carapace limit its movement, but if disturbed, it can still use its caudal fin and can be unexpectedly quick.

D – The great gorgonian sea fans, which grow on the walls of the reef, offer shelter and nourishment to a dense swarm of fish. The photo shows a butterflyfish (Chaetodon fasciatus).

C

D

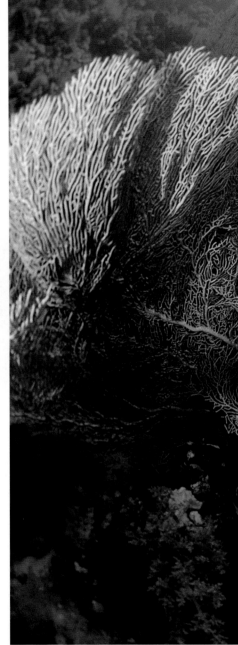

A – The splendid fans of the giant gorgonians of the Red Sea offer support to other life forms as well. In this case, a crinoid takes advantage of the position exposed to the current to capture plankton to feed on.

the Baraka, which flows into the Sudan, makes the waters more limpid and transparent than any other on earth, with sunlight penetrating to significant depths. This means that anyone equipped with a mask and flippers can explore this immense expanse of coral teeming with life. In fact, the greatest attraction for snorkeling fans is the coastal reef, with vertical walls that plunge from the surface to the most inaccessible depths, like slopes draped with cascades of branched coral, intricate formations of gorgonians and delicate tufts of *Alcyonaria* in a thousand colors. A spectacular variety of marine fauna swims among the reef structures, from little purple anthias to green chromis, brightly colored butterflyfish to comical pufferfish, *Labridae* from the little cleaner wrasse to the enormous humphead wrasse, and surgeonfish to curious parrotfish. They all find shelter and food in this underwater jungle, through a complex food chain. Different defense behaviors and feeding strategies allow diverse organisms to share the same area. They all have the same objectives for survival: occupy a territory and defend it, and feed and reproduce under optimal conditions to guarantee the continuity of the species. This whole system follows millenary rules and codes that only external factors, such as the inconsiderate behavior of humans toward the sea, can alter or destroy.

Swimming suspended above the Red Sea coral reef is like flying in absolute silence over a planet populated by strange, colorful creatures who often approach us curiously, welcoming us to their odd and fascinating world.

F

E – A timid spotted hawkfish (Cirrhitichthys oxycephalus) resting on a soft layer of soft corals. Snorkelers can observe an infinite variety of scenes in the life of the coral reef.

F – During the day, small gray morays (Siderea grisea) stay near their dens. They come out after sunset to hunt, aided by the sense of smell.

Potential hazards

Snorkeling has some potential risks, but anyone with some experience in tropical seas knows that any harm caused by contact with animals is always the result of the swimmer's inconsiderate behavior. A scorpionfish (*Scorpaenopsis barbatus*) or fire coral (*Millepora dichotoma*) will never leave the sea bed to attack or sting a swimmer on the surface! Animals react only when provoked or when they sense danger, so never touch anything that you find underwater. The potential danger lies not in large predators like sharks, despite sensational movies featuring imaginary monsters, but rather in small animals that can poison or sting. The most dangerous species certainly belong to the scorpionfish family, and they are also the hardest to identify because of their mimetic capabilities. There are 35 known species of scorpionfish, including *Pterois volitans* and radiata, certainly the most obvious due to their feather-like fins and peculiar coloration, and the stonefish

(*Synanceia verrucosa*), a true quick-change artist that can take on the color and characteristics of the floor on which it rests. While the first two can inflict extremely painful stings with their dorsal and lateral plumes, causing fevers that can be somewhat serious, the poison of an adult stonefish can be lethal. All these fish can inject neurotoxic poisons that cause symptoms such as acute pain, tachycardia, conspicuous local swelling and excessive sweating, accompanied by fever. The individual reactivity of the person bitten makes it difficult to quantify the exact extent of the damage done. It's important to know that neurotoxins are thermolabile poisons; that is, they are dispersed by heat. An application of hot packs on the bite will neutralize much of the poison. So you need to be very careful not to stand on the reef, and absolutely avoid walking on the reef emerging from the surface. Even the colorful crown-of-thorns (*Acanthaster planci*), one of the most beautiful starfish you can admire, can cause painful stings with the sharp stingers on its numerous arms. In this case as well, you can apply hot water to the wound, which will swell rapidly. Sea urchins also have long spines that can easily prick the skin, causing great pain. One of the (sadly) best known stinging species is the fire coral (*Millepora dichotoma*), a colony of coelenterates that looks like stiff yellow-ocher fans with white tips. If touched, this hydrozoan, a distant relation of the jellyfish, produces extensive burns caused by nematocysts, microscopic algae that inject a poison that causes redness and very irritating erythremia. If you come in contact with this coral, which is omnipresent in the shallower portion of the reef, the best first aid relief is to wash

and energetically rub the injured part with sea water and then apply a cortisone cream to the area. Cone shells should never be touched either, as they have a mobile organ similar to a blowgun that shoots a poisonous dart which can cause muscular paralysis. Remember that gathering shells is absolutely prohibited. This includes even dead shells, which may still hold some unpleasant surprises! Morays look quite fierce, with their open mouths armed with sharp teeth. They are actually no real danger, but may become aggressive if greatly disturbed. Watch them, and you'll see that they are splendid animals that often come curiously out of their dens to watch you. While they're totally harmless unless you unexpectedly try to touch them, the bite of a moray will give you a permanent scar. Abrasions and cuts from contact with coral can become infected if not cared for properly. Disinfect all cuts you get in the ocean, and if the cut is large, avoid getting it wet. Remember that if you inadvertently touch any coral, it can not only have unpleasant consequences for you, but will irreparably damage the coral.

A – A hawkfish (Paracirrhites forsteri) on a formation of fire corals (Millepora dichotoma). *Touching one of these little branches is painful and will cause a serious skin rash.*

B – The crown-of-thorns (Acanthaster planci) has numerous arms with spines that will inject a painful poison if touched.

C – This stonefish (Synanceia verrucosa) resting on the seabed mimics its surroundings and becomes invisible.

D – Another quick-change artists living hidden on the sea floor is the scorpionfish (Scorpaenopsis oxycephala).

E – Even sea urchins (Diadema setosum) have spines that can

pierce the skin and break off under it, causing painful inflammations.

F – The Pterois is one of the most dangerous creatures your will encounter in your excursions on the water's surface.

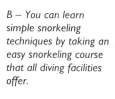

A, C – The movement that allows you to go from swimming on the surface to a dive underwater is a somersault known as a "flip turn." This movement will bring the weight of your legs up vertically onto your head and carry your whole body underwater. When your flippers are also immersed, you can start pushing and reach the desired depth. So don't forget to compensate for hydrostatic pressure!

B – You can learn simple snorkeling techniques by taking an easy snorkeling course that all diving facilities offer.

D – Just dive in a few meters below the surface and you'll become part of the new, fascinating world of the Red Sea coral reefs.

Many people think that snorkeling is so easy that you need no training or knowledge, but that's not exactly how it is!

In addition to learning how to put on and use the equipment, you should know a few simple principles of physics and heat regulation to fully enjoy this fantastic, entertaining activity that can add some excitement to your tropical vacation. Snorkeling is certainly the easiest and most relaxing way to explore a world as diverse and fascinating as the coral reef. The word "snorkel" is actually a neologism used to describe any tube used to take in air and expel it under the surface of the water when necessary, but it is now used primarily to describe the equipment that allows a human to swim without lifting his head to breathe. It comes from the German *Schnorkel*, the device used by submarines to take in fresh air while navigating at periscope level, and now means an aerator for surface respiration. So what exactly does a snorkeler do? He swims on the surface of the water, breathing through an aerator (i.e. through the mouth and not the nose, as he would in an air environment) and, through the glass front of his mask, observes life below the surface of the water. Snorkeling has thus become a basic

offering of tropical vacation villages for anyone who's not too confident in the sea and doesn't have a license that would allow him to dive with breathing apparatus, but doesn't want to give up the joy of observing what's happening under the surface of the sea. Let's look at the environmental and physiological conditions of someone in the water. First of all, contrary to what many believe, people float. All you have to do is fill your lungs with air to float effortlessly on the surface of the water. If a person on the water's surface breathes calmly through the snorkel with his nose closed by the mask, he can float without moving a muscle! The problem is water temperature. Human beings have an average temperature of 36-37°C, which is maintained by the metabolic activity of the cells. In the water, the body cools 25 times faster than in air, so you need to protect yourself to avoid excessive heat loss. For this, all you need to do is wear a tight neoprene wetsuit that will not only minimize heat loss, but also protect the body from accidental abrasions and harsh sunlight. They come in a special blend of very soft, thermal, synthetic rubber 1 to 5 mm thick. Mammals and marine reptiles have evolved their underwater vision using a device called a nictitating membrane that creates a sort of transparent air chamber around the eyes, allowing them to clearly see underwater.

Human eyes, however, are not designed for underwater vision. We need to bring a bubble of air for our eyes in order to recreate the air environment and give the eye its normal refracting power. For this reason we have to wear a mask. The mask may be in rubber or silicon, preferably the latter because of its robustness and long wear. It needs to be soft and adhere perfectly to the contours of the face, the glass must be tempered, and the mask should be easy to adjust even while being worn.

A

B

The mask should cover the nose, and no swimming goggles may be used. For people with vision problems, there are masks available on the market that have corrective lenses gauged to every need. The flippers are your propulsion system and should be extremely comfortable to wear. If your flippers are too tight or too loose, they can create a number of problems. A pair of light neoprene shoes are recommended to better protect your feet. The length of the paddle depends on how you want to use it, and the material should float if you accidentally lose it in the water. If you're not very confident in the water, a floating device consisting of an inflatable vest will keep you on the surface with no problem.

As in any other recreational activity, the quality of your equipment will be important if you want to enjoy snorkeling. Buying snorkeling equipment may seem very easy, but you really need to keep some fundamental criteria in mind to be sure you've made the right purchase. First of all, realize that the money you spend on equipment is an investment in safety and pleasure. After safety, comfort should be your second criterion for selection. The time spent in a shop ensuring that the underwater equipment fits your body and is appropriate for its intended use is thus fundamental for enjoyable dives.

C

A, B – Snorkelers usually stay on the surface or only a few meters deep, where the water temperature is higher. A thermal neoprene wetsuit is necessary to protect you.

C – A good mask is indispensable if you want to be comfortable in the water. A mask that does not fit the face perfectly can create discomfort and annoying leaks.

D - Snorkeling is fun and allows those who are not confident in the sea to *enjoy the beauty that the underwater worlds of our planet offer.*

E – The movement of your flippers on the surface stirs up large quantities of plankton particles on which small fish feed. The snorkeler in the picture, seen flippering, is followed by a great number of sergeant majors (Abudefduf saxatillis) that find nourishment thanks to this unusual movement of water.

D

SHARM EL-SHEIKH

A

The Sinai Peninsula is shaped like a formless upside-down triangle whose southern tip comprises the Ras Mohammed promontory. At the extreme south of this imposing watershed that wedges into the Red Sea, forming the Gulf of Suez to the east and the Gulf of Aqaba to the west, is one of the most famous marine areas on the Egyptian coast: Sharm el-Sheikh.

In Arabic, Sharm el-Sheikh means "Sheik's bay." It was discovered by Israeli tourists during the Israeli occupation in the 1960s. By the mid-eighties, the rapid transformation of a peaceful Bedouin village into a metropolis of international tourism had begun. Today, heading north from the bay of Sharm el-Maya, you'll see dozens of tourist facilities (which often clash with the surrounding landscape), and the coast has been paved up to the littoral zone across from Tiran Island. The first city, established in 1968, was the present-day Sharm el-Sheikh, a town on the bay of El-Maya. It has numerous hotels, a number of typical restaurants where you can enjoy local cuisine, and a folk bazaar with a good selection of handicrafts. Not far off is El-Mina, one of the two ports of embarkation in the area, a starting point for daily

A – The stone door is a symbolic boundary to the entrance of the Ras Mohammed National Park. It was created in 1983 to protect the ecosystem that extends to the southernmost portion of the Sinai Peninsula.

B – Until a short time ago, the bay of Sharm el-Maya was a departure point for boats bringing tourists to the coast every day. Another port is now used for water craft, and perhaps Sharm Bay will be restored to its former condition in a few years.

Far Garden

Naama Bay

Near Garden

SHARM EL-SHEIKH

Temple

Ras Umm Sid

RAS MOHAMMED NATIONAL PARK

Marsa Bareka

RAS MOHAMMED

B

Ras Mohammed

The Quay

Jackson Reef

Gordon Reef

Ras Bob

White Knight

TIRAN ISLAND

E

C

D

C, D – Along the walls of the reef are incredible concentrations of alcyonarians, forming a palette of a thousand colors. Moreover, the gorgonians reach spectacular dimensions that testify to the great biodiversity of the Red Sea.

E – The currents of the Gulf of Suez and the Gulf of Aqaba meet along the southern coasts of the Sinai, attracting dense swarms of predators like these trevallies (Caranx sp.).

excursions to the Sinai coast. Six kilometers farther north is Naama Bay, with large hotels, shopping centers and all the infrastructures necessary for a vacation area. This is the area that has changed the most, and now that the coastline is filled up, hotels are being built inland near the desert.

A third tourist/hotel center has developed on the Ras Umm Sid plateau between El-Maya and Naama, the two best known areas. Hundreds of structures and dwellings have changed the face of what was one of the most interesting natural marine areas in the entire Red Sea. You can dive from the beaches and sea approaches of the various hotels and begin to explore the surface areas of the coastal coral reef. This area is gradually losing its stony corals, but fish life is still rather interesting. Nevertheless, the most fascinating reefs are always far from the daily assault of bathers, who in complete ignorance believe that the coral reef is nothing more than a lifeless underwater mountain. The best preserved destinations are the shallow beds around the four reefs between the east coast of the Sinai Peninsula and Tiran Island. They're in an ideal position in terms of the currents that carry in plankton and thus nourishment, and you'll find dense clusters of alcyonarians on the underwater walls, associated with true forests of gorgonians. These coral reefs and those in the Ras Mohammed Marine Park district in northern Egypt have the greatest wealth of marine life.

JACKSON REEF

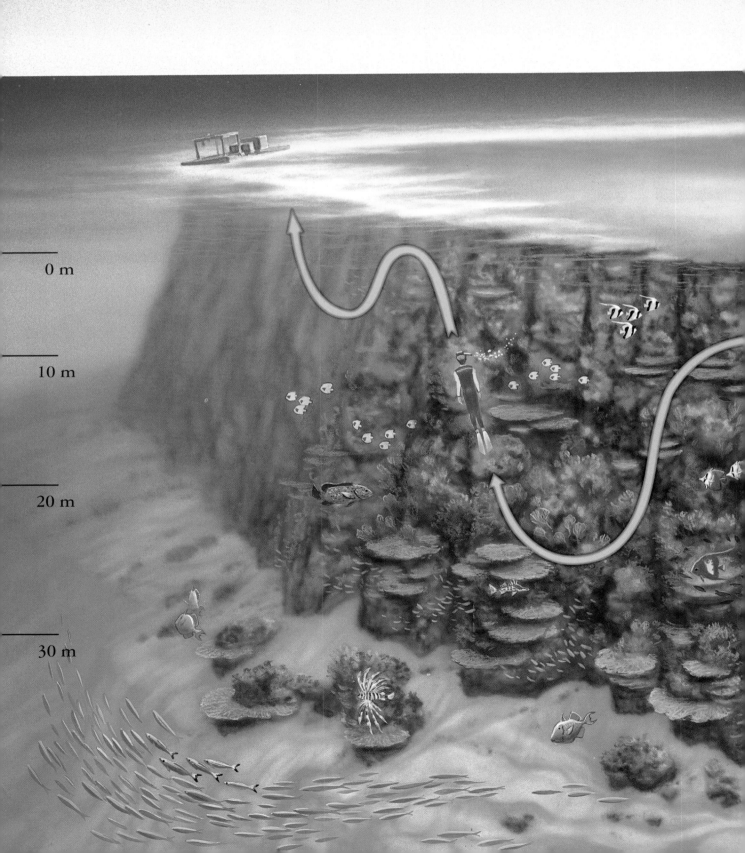

0 m

10 m

20 m

30 m

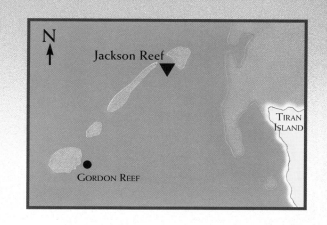

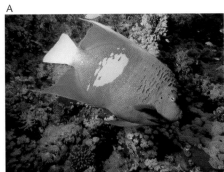

A

A – The yellowband angelfish (Pomacanthus maculosus) *can be recognized by the white spot on its side. It leads a solitary life and only joins other members of its species during the mating period.*

B – The blue triggerfish (Pseudobalistes fuscus) *in search of its favorite food: sea urchins. It has an odd technique for overcoming the obstacle of the urchin's long spines: it rolls them over with a powerful jet of water so it can reach the oral disk.*

Four semi-emerged coral reefs lie between the Sinai coast and the island of Tiran. Jackson, the northernmost reef, can be reached in little over an hour by sailing north from the tourist harbor at Naama Bay. The coral formation, which is more or less circular, is marked by a lighthouse on the east side, while to the north the remains of a shipwreck are a reminder that this is the reef most exposed to winds and currents, making the well-protected, tranquil southern side the best place to explore. Even from the surface, the sea's myriad shades of color, from the dark blue of the deeper waters to the delicate azure of the lagoon, are a truly astonishing spectacle. Put on your mask and flippers and jump off the back platform of the boat, and you'll soon come to the reef. Here you'll have a taste of what you can expect: a large school of blue and yellow fusiliers (*Caesio suevica*) swims peacefully below the boat, not intimidated in the slightest by the endless procession of divers. Surgeonfish ceaselessly go from the reef to the keel of the boats, where they pull off the encrusted algae. If you're especially lucky, you may be greeted by a large humphead wrasse who lives permanently in

C - This coral pinnacle has been completely colonized by soft corals. The position, exposed to currents carrying in nutrients, is ideal for the maximum growth of these alcyonarians.

these waters and will come almost close enough to touch. But resist the temptation, because your hands would remove the mucous that protects its surface, thus creating fragile areas that may be attacked by parasites that could cause serious harm. The wall, which drops straight down to a depth of almost 50 meters, is quite broken even at the surface, with deep cracks that let you enter the lagoon at high tide. Don't do this at any other time or you may damage the reef and injure yourself too, as the corals are quite sharp. The reef is a true explosion of life and color: the abundant nutrients carried in by the

B

C

E

D

constant currents have encouraged the growth of enormous alcyonarians with bright colors running from pink to fuchsia to red, with thousands of marine organisms living within its branches. The lovely emperor angelfish (*Pomacanthus imperator*) and half moon angelfish (*Pomacanthus maculosus*) are regular inhabitants of this area. Swimming tranquilly in this coral garden, you can also see beautiful yellowedge lyretails (*Variola louti*) and red coral groupers (*Cephalopholis miniata*) who scour the territory in search of small fish and crustaceans. You'll see *Pterois volitans* perched on delicate branches of gorgonians, almost as if they're resting, tired of incessantly swimming. A myriad of sea anemones have found a place between an *Acropora* coral and an alcyonarian, living in symbiosis with a pair of combative clownfish (*Amphiprion bicinctus*): it's quite interesting to see how these little fish defend their home. The wall, which you should

D – The lower part of the umbrella of this Acropora offers shelter to a beautiful saddleback grouper (Plectropomus pessuliferus). This grouper, which may reach one meter in length, at times joins others of its species in coordinated hunting activity.

E – A small nudibranch (Chromodoris quadricolor) is greedily feeding on the tissues of this beautiful red sponge (Latrunculia corticata). Despite the fact that they are rather easy to observe, we know little about this species.

A – In the rich waters of Jackson Reef, just below the surface of the sea, you can see dense schools of fish living together, like these two-banded porgies (Acanthopagus bifasciatus) swimming tranquilly with a school of emperors (Lethrinus nebulosus).

B – One of the most exciting encounters on detrital floors is certainly with invertebrates like this Alicia. Its delicate structure and the undulating tuft of tentacles are an unforgettable sight.

C - Sponges often enter into competition with corals: to create space for themselves, they may even emit acid substances that dissolve limestone.

A

keep to your right during your exploration, is so full of life that you should examine it at a leisurely pace, because any small area may reveal many forms of life. Timid hawkfish (Oxycirrhites typus) live among the tangled branches of the gorgonians, along with pipefish who are quite mimetic so that they can more easily hunt the small crustaceans on which they subsist. The brightly colored butterflyfish move incessantly from one coral formation to another, feasting on coral polyps. When frightened, blue triggerfish quickly take refuge in the first crevice they find, leaving only their tails exposed.

B

It's quite common to see sea turtles (Chelonia mydas) swimming peacefully along the reef, heading to the surface to take a breath of air. As the reef is more exposed to the current, you should always look out to the abyss to glimpse groups of trevallies and tunas, ceaselessly on the prowl, and you may even see a truly breathtaking sight: a whitetip shark. You can finish your exploration in the lagoon, where the shallow waters and bright sunlight create beautiful patterns of light, and the sandy bottom, which may seem lifeless at first glance, holds extraordinary forms of life. You may spot lizardfish (Saurida gracilis) camouflaged on the floor, patiently waiting for a fish to carelessly come

C

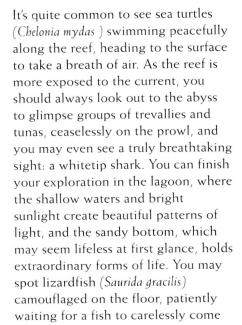

too close, small gobies (Amblyeleotris steinitzi) who share their dens in a symbiotic relationship with the Alpheus shrimp, or large sea cucumbers moving slowly on the floor, ingesting detritus and extracting the organic substances on which they feed.

So move very carefully even when no form of life seems to be present, because the entire marine world is an extremely fragile ecosystem that should always be respected. Don't go into the water in places where you'll have to walk on the reef!!

D

D – In one small dive, this snorkeler can get a close-up look at this school of bigeye emperors (Monotaxis grandoculis), *which hover almost motionless in the water during the day.*

E – *The characteristic color and elongated snout make this hawkfish (Oxycirrhites typus) easy to identify. Hawkfish are common in red gorgonians, among whose branches they camouflage themselves with incredible skill.*

E

GORDON REEF

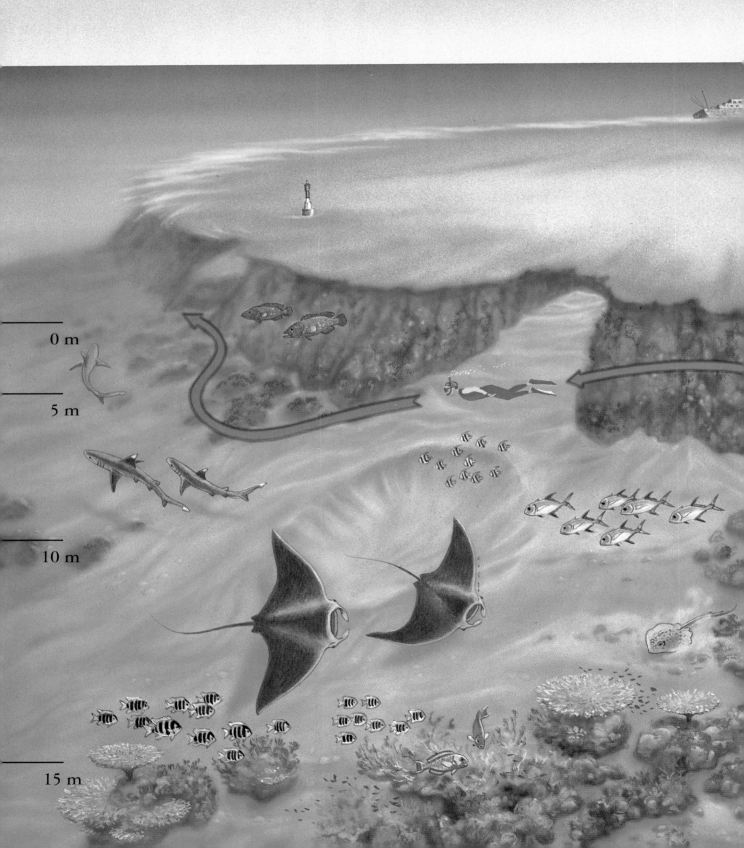

0 m

5 m

10 m

15 m

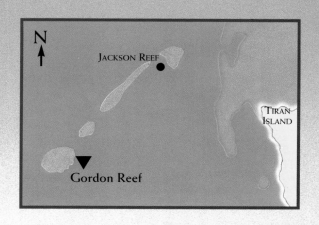

JACKSON REEF

TIRAN
ISLAND

Gordon Reef

N

A

A – At Gordon Reef, sheltered from winds and currents, you can admire all the splendor of the explosion of life in this stretch of reef.

B – Four reefs stand in a line across from Tiran Island, dividing the Aqaba channel into two branches and making navigation perilous, as testified by the shipwreck which ran aground in the northern part of Gordon Reef.

C – The red coral grouper (Cephalopholis miniata) defends its territory. It belongs to a harem of one male and a group of females.

D – Pterois miles sometimes abandon the crevices where they lie waiting for a prey and circle about in the open water.

E – In the upper portion of the reef, the light makes coral growth more luxuriant.

F – A trevally (Caranx sp.) seems to seek the protection of this humpback wrasse (Cheilinus undulatus). The latter is characterized by a horn on the front of the head, which is only present in older, larger individuals, and a snout distinguished by a dense reticulum.

B

Gordon is one of four reefs located between the Sinai coast and Turan Island. It is the southernmost reef and the first you'll encounter about an hour's sail from Naama Bay.

Especially in the morning, sea conditions are not optimal due to the wind that blows ceaselessly in this area for most of the year. Sometimes even the current can be annoying, and you need to be very careful not to go too far from the boat: the swim back against the current would be anything but pleasant! This circular, semi-emerged coral agglomerate is easy to identify because in 1981 a merchant ship foundered on the reef, where it remained trapped in an upright position. The contour of the reef is broken by inlets with sandy floors that connect the open sea to the shallow lagoons, which you can only enter during high tide. It's one of the best sites for snorkeling, as you'll immediately note from the riot of colors the sea offers. The deep blue sea fades into pale azure where the sandy bottom reflects the bright sunlight. The anchoring shamandura (special mooring lines) are all at the southern side of the reef, which is the most sheltered from the wind and currents, so your adventure should begin in this area. As soon as you drop into the water, you'll be surrounded by a blaze of colors and marine forms. The first thing you'll see is a humphead wrasse (Cheilinus undulatus) who is a permanent resident here. He will approach you fearlessly, perhaps recalling the hard-boiled eggs some ignorant human gave him. You should never, ever feed the marine animals, first of all because giving them food that they don't

E

customarily eat could kill them, and secondly because this alters their behavior and makes them more aggressive. Always show respect for this world, where you are only a temporary visitor! The sea floor, which descends to a depth of 10 meters from the surface in a gentle slope, is completely covered with corals of every kind,

C

D

which thrive due to the current that brings them an abundance of nutritious substances. There are alcyonarians in the midst of which swim thousands of anthias (*Pseudanthias squamipinnis*), red coral groupers (*Ceohalopholis miniata*) defending their territory, butterflyfish who ceaselessly seek coral polyps, hard corals whose calcareous support is crumbled by the sturdy beak of the parrotfish, and gorgonians with branches that hide timid hawkfish (*Oxycirrhites typus*) and elegant *Volitans*. Right below the surface you can see schools of cornetfish (*Fistularia commersonii*), silvery, tapered

A

D

B

C

trumpetfish that swim alongside you, and groups of comical-looking sergeant majors (*Abudefduf sexatilis*), who appear to be wearing white and black striped pajamas. The sandy and detrital areas of the sea floor are the realm of the ever-present bluespotted ribbontail rays (*Taeniura lymma*), who scour the flat surfaces in search of food. You're likely to see some sea turtles as well (*Chelonia mydas*), who ignore the traffic of boats and people and graze peacefully in a "field" of especially tasty sponges. As the snorkeling area is in the middle of the Strait of Gobal and is swept by currents, an encounter with large pelagic creatures is not unlikely. From time to time gaze out to sea to glimpse a whitefin shark, large *Plectropomus* groupers just below the surface examining the wall for possible prey, and schools of trevallies who tirelessly patrol the reef. During the spring, if you're especially lucky you may also see the elegant maneuvers of a marine giant, the manta. While you're immersed in this fantastic world, always be careful not to venture too close to the reef, which you could inadvertently damage with your flippers.

At some times of year this area is quite crowded, and you'll need to be very careful when returning to the boat after your "stroll" across the surface. Be sure there are no moving boats nearby, and always avoid swimming between two moored boats, as a wave could throw them together and seriously injure you.

E F G

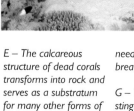

A – The flexible structure of gorgonians is due to the lack of calcification in the skeleton.

B – The trevallies (Caranx sexfasciatus) like to hunt almost at the water surface.

C – Rays (Manta birostris) are harmless creatures that feed on plankton.

D – Older, sicker fish in the school of yellowfin goatfish (Mulloides vanicolensis) are positioned on the outside of the school in order to protect younger, healthy fish from a possible attack.

E – The calcareous structure of dead corals transforms into rock and serves as a substratum for many other forms of life.

F – Despite the fact that they have evolved to be perfectly adapted to marine life, turtles still need the outside world to breathe and reproduce.

G – The bluespotted stingray (Taeniura lymma) camouflages itself by covering itself with a thin layer of sand. Sandy and detrital areas are the best places to spot one of these creatures.

RAS BOB

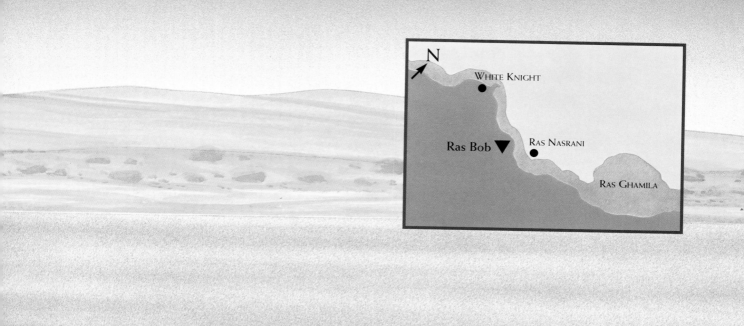

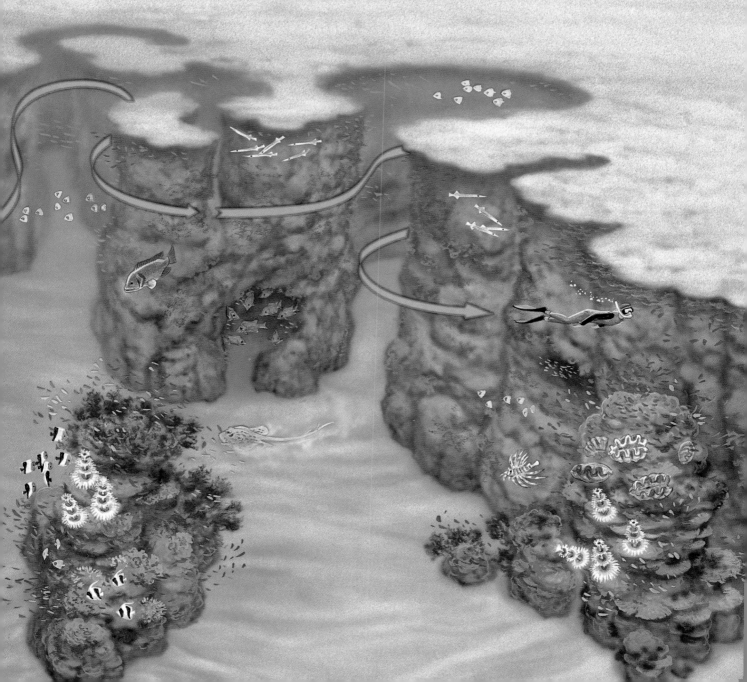

WHITE KNIGHT

Ras Bob ▼   Ras Nasrani

RAS GHAMILA

A

eaving from the Naama
Bay dock, in a little under
an hour you can sail to
one of the loveliest places on the
coast north of Sharm. Ras Bob is an
inlet well-sheltered from the north
winds and waves, making it an
ideal place for snorkelers to
explore. A beautiful beach runs
across the whole bay. Until
recently, it was a reproduction area
for turtles, but now, unfortunately,
it has become the destination of
dozens of visitors staying in the
hotel that has been built here. The
arm of sea facing the beach is still
frequented by a few turtles who
remember that tongue of sand, but
now it's no longer suitable for
depositing the precious eggs that
ensure the survival of its species.
There are mooring lines for the
boats, and in my opinion, the one
in the middle is the best, as it
makes it easy to visit the reef both
east and west of the mooring
point. From the surface, the wall
drops to a depth of 4-6 meters
onto a sandy floor that slopes
down gently to a depth of 20
meters, then plunges off into the
deep blue sea. The wall that runs
from the surface forms small inlets
with floors of pure white sand,
creating natural swimming pools
where you can swim tranquilly.

B

This bank is broken by a number of
small caves filled with swarms of
glassfish (*Parapriacanthus guentheri*)
intent on escaping their mortal
enemy, the redmouth grouper
(*Aethaloperca rogaa*). The rays of light
that penetrate these fissures,
striking these silvery lovers of

Sharm el-Sheikh

A – As the wall at Ras Bob is 4-5 meters deep, it is easy to admire the reef.

B – Imposing formations of fire coral have grown in the area. Be careful not to touch Hydroids, which will burn your skin.

C – There are caverns a few meters below the surface where the sunlight penetrates, creating lovely reflections on the sandy floor.

D – A pair of clownfish (Amphiprion bicinctus) patrol their territory, never going too far from the anemone that hosts them.

E – A redmouth grouper (Aethaloperca rogaa) watches over its hunting territory. These voracious carnivores prey on glassfish, which can be seen in the lower part of the image.

C

D

who flee to the safety of their branches at the first sign of danger. Another rather common stony coral formation is the *Porites genus*, with interesting life forms that colonize the open areas left when coral polyps die, making them look like a bright bed of flowers. There are brilliant giant clams that owe their bright colors to algae, and curious, multihued worms that resemble Christmas trees *(Spirobranchus giganteus)*, who disappear into their calcareous tube at the slightest movement in the water. Although this coral formation may look like a rock, it is a living thing and grows very slowly, less than a centimeter a year, so be very careful not to damage its delicate structure by striking it with the tip of your flippers. Given the abundance of corals, there are also many butterflyfish who greedily pull off the coral polyps with their beaks. It's interesting to note how representatives of almost all species live in pairs. Just below the surface of this tranquil stretch of sea, small schools of cornetfish *(Fistularia commersonii)* float motionless, rocked gently by the peaceful backwash, while schools of sergeant majors move continuously in a frenetic bustle, approaching you fearlessly, representatives of a world that has so many thrilling sensations to offer.

twilight, creates truly lovely sights. Another fish that has taken up residence in these caves is the squirrelfish, which is nocturnal and gathers in small groups in these shadowy areas. Small coral pinnacles rise from the detrital plateau, offering an excellent support for small brown gorgonians and soft coral formations in odd broccoli-like shapes, surrounded by small bright red anthias that add a cheerful touch. The shallow water and bright sunlight striking the sea floor make it possible to spot crocodile fish *(Papilloculiceps longiceps)* skillfully camouflaged among the sediment, lying in wait

for some small fish or crustacean, which they'll catch in a rapid jerk. Another common visitor to this type of floor is the bluespotted ribbontail ray *(Taeniura lymma)*. Lying immobile sheltered among the coral formations, it will not hesitate to flee if you come too close. You can see *Pterois volitans* among the coral formations, seeking shelter until twilight, when they'll come out to hunt. Stony corals are well represented by numerous species that include *Acropora* corals. Their intricate, delicate branches offer protection to numerous organisms, including small crabs and schools of chromis

E

WHITE KNIGHT

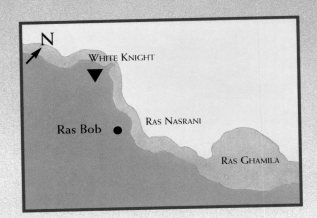

N

White Knight

Ras Nasrani

Ras Bob

Ras Ghamila

0 m

5 m

10 m

15 m

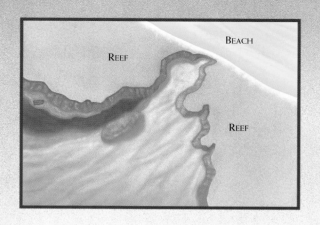

REEF

BEACH

REEF

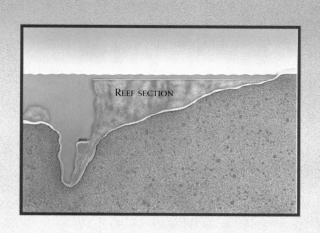

REEF SECTION

A – The complex structure of Turbinaria corals is the result of the need to expose as much surface area as possible to light.

B – A small crustacean has settled in the empty shell of a Gasteropod.

C – Compact swarms of yellowsaddle goatfish can be seen against the wall (Parupeneus cyclostomus).

D – The wall of the reef hosts large predators of the barrier reef such as the spotted grouper (Plectropomus pessuliferus).

E – Two morays (Gymnothorax javanicus) *peeping out of the same den. These members of the order Anguilliformes come out only at night to hunt.*

Departing from the pier at Naama Bay and sailing north for about 40 minutes, you'll come to little White Knight Bay. The inlet is well-sheltered from the north winds, and the reef is broken by a small beach, across from which you can tie your boat to the mooring line. These lines can be found all along the coast of the Sharm el-Sheikh district and act as anchoring points for the boats that visit the area daily. They are an excellent way to protect an ecosystem as important and fragile as this. The sandy beach continues underwater, where you can begin your excursion with mask and flippers. Dozens of eels live on this sandy plateau, and you can see them floating at the water's surface, where they capture food carried in by the current. Seen from above, they look like reeds blown by the wind, but they'll hasten to take shelter underground if they sense the slightest danger. Proceed by

going toward the boat, then, keeping the coastline to your right, you'll come to the canyon, a deep cleft in the reef. From above, it looks like a wound traversing the sea floor, starting at a depth of 10 meters and dropping down to 40. It's a truly lovely sight, as the white sand on the bottom reflects the sunlight in a thousand sparkling patterns of light.

On one side of the canyon is a unique stony coral formation that looks like an enormous green cabbage: it's a colony of *Turbinaria mesenterina* over two meters in diameter. A myriad of small marine organisms lives among its laminae, which seem to be stacked up untidily. There are small blennies that find shelter among its leaves, fantastically colored *Spirobranchus giganteus* worms that look like so many colorful Christmas trees, and small giant clams (*Tridacna gigas*) who find this a firm substratum to

F – An angelfish (Pomacanthus maculosus) *around a coral pinnacle in search of edible sponges. They form pairs only during the mating season.*

G – This colorful image shows a pair of nudibranchs (Chomodoris quadricolor) *moving slowly along a beautiful, bright red sponge.*

F

G

which they can attach. These mollusks get their bright colors from numerous algae, known as zooxanthellae, which also provide a significant quantity of nutritive substances. Continuing your exploration, you'll see that the wall is covered with soft corals (*Tubipora musica*) that look like so many flowers continuously opening and closing. A vast variety of *Chaetodontidae*, or butterflyfish, "graze" on this white flower bed, greedy for coral polyps. It's not uncommon to see even half moon angelfish (*Pomacanthus maculosus*), in my opinion one of the most beautiful fish to live in this sea. It's an extremely curious creature and

may well come quite close to examine you, but it's also quick to flee. Yellowsaddle goatfish (*Parupeneus cyclostomus*) can be seen in the small spaces not covered by coral formations. These fish scour the floor in search of the small fish on which they feed, inserting their long barbels under the sand to find them. You can often see families of young humphead wrasses (*Cheilinus undulatus*) in this area, easily recognizable by not only their form, but their light gray color, as they pass by quickly in single file. They're much less sociable than adult wrasses and quite hard to approach. This is one of the few areas where you can find an extremely unusual sea anemone. Its tentacles, which end in a bubble, are a beautiful red color, and as usual house a family of clownfish (*Amphiprion bicinctus*). Still keeping the wall to your right, you'll come to a small wreck of a day boat that sank after a fire. The wreck is fairly

D

E

recent, so the body of the craft has not yet been encrusted by many marine organisms, but the stern has already been colonized by a cloud of glassfish (*Parapriacanthus guentheri*), in the midst of which live a pair of *Pterois volitans*, which have cleverly decided to live in the pantry.

The prow of the wreck has become home to a moray (*Gymnothorax javanicus*) and a beautiful grouper (*Plectropomus pessuliferus*) which, immobile on the planking, is very probably engrossed in having cleaner wrasses (*Labroides dimidiatus*) remove parasites. When you come to this wreck, it unfortunately means that it's time to end your exploration and return to the boat.

A

B

C

A – An anemone is almost suffocated by a tuft of Alcyonaria. Some corals secrete toxic substances to inhibit the growth of other species.

B – Batfish (Platax teira) are more commonly seen in the morning.

C – A cleaner shrimp is taking care of a moray. Cleaners have a symbiotic relationship with their hosts.

D – A whitespotted grouper (Epinephelus summana) takes shelter in the wreckage of a ship that sank in the White Knight area.

E – Two scorpionfish (Scorpaenopsis oxycephala) were photographed in the act of performing a courting ritual.

F – Swarms of glassfish (Parapriacanthus guentheri) dart away to shelter within the reassuring mass of gorgonians.

0 m

5 m

N

NAAMA BAY

Far Garden

CORAL BAY

N

REEF

A

B

C

A – Near the beach of Naama Bay, large blooms of Alcyonaria are embellished by necklaces of anthias.

B – A snorkeler nears the gulf where the Gardens of Naama are located.

C – This odd-looking Canthigaster valentini is a member of the pufferfish family. It is very timid, always swims next to the reef and is rarely seen in the open water.

small vertical wall, then continues with a plateau that gently slopes down to a depth of 25 meters, where it finally drops off into the blue abyss. This portion of reef that extends out to the open sea is swept by constant currents that carry in abundant nutrients to benthic marine organisms, who have found ideal conditions for creating a true garden. From the plateau, which has a sandy bottom, lovely coral towers rise almost to the surface and are covered with soft corals in vivid colors that form multihued palettes. Here you will find scalefin anthias (*Pseudanthias squamipinnis*) whose incessant movements are proof of how active underwater life can be. The walls of these pinnacles are an

D – The feathery bushes (Macrorhynchia philippina) *on top of this coral tower belong to the class of Hydrozoans*, close relatives of the fire coral.

E – A squirrelfish (Sargocentron spiniferum) *stays in the shade of a large umbrella built by the polyps of an Acropora.*

F – This flame parrotfish (Scarus ghobban) *can also be found in sandy areas far from the reed. In addition to normal horny dental plates, adult males also have two canine teeth on the upper jaw.*

Far Garden is the northern tip of the great bay that surrounds the Naama Bay beach and the northernmost coral garden. It's a short sail from the Naama pier. This Garden is located farther from the great hotel complexes on the bay, so it's less crowded, and its fortunate geographical position, sheltered from the north winds, has made it one of the best places for snorkeling. Here as well, there are two mooring lines where you can tie your boat and make your exploration more convenient. The reef drops perpendicularly from the surface for 4-5 meters in a

ideal support for stony corals, in whose contorted branches clouds of green chromis (*Chromis viridis*) and small blennies find refuge. The blennies motionlessly survey their territory, but they'll vanish in an instant at any hint of danger. Gaudy parrotfish are everywhere. They move continuously along the reef, using their sturdy beaks to scrape the surface of large corals to remove the algae from them. It's also common to see the comical-looking pufferfish (*Arothron diadematosus*), whose black mask across its eyes makes it look like a bandit, wandering among the *Acropora* corals and using its

A — *The long branches of red whip coral (Ellisella sp.) reach out to the sun. A close inspection among the filaments will reveal numerous small animals that find protection in the tangled mass.*

B — *Glassfish (Parapricanthus guentheri) can commonly be found under the protrusions of the wall or at the base of gorgonian fans. These fish are not fond of light and prefer shadowy areas.*

C — *Alcyonaria come in many forms, sizes and colors. With favorable environmental conditions, they can proliferate and colonize vast areas of the reef.*

D — *A turtle resting on the floor seems to be watching a group of batfish (Platax orbicularis).*

A

sturdy beak to pull off the tips of the branches. At the base of these stony coral formations, on the sandy floor, blue-spotted stingrays (*Taeniura lymma*) half-buried in the sand patiently await the best time to begin their hunting. Always remember to glance out to the open sea, because as you're near a

point, and thus an area swept by currents, you may see bands of dentex (*Luthjanus bohar*) motionless near the surface, constantly surveying their hunting territory, or trevallies keeping an eye on a school of fusiliers (*Caesio suevicus*), ready to move in as soon as the school lets down its defenses. As you return to the boat, explore the wall that runs from the surface to a depth of about 5 meters, offering truly thrilling sights. The cracks that break the wall create an endless pattern of light produced by the sun and the thousands of shimmering glassfish that live sheltered in these caves, waiting for night to fall, when they come

C

out near the reef to hunt the zooplankton on which they feed.

You can also see groups of soldierfish, who prefer to shelter in shadowy areas during the day. Little cavities become the dens of gray morays (*Siderea grisea*), which are easy to find because they live in shallow waters. You may even see one in its own den. Right below the surface are large groups of sergeant majors (*Abudefduf vaigiensis*), and if you move very cautiously, you may be able to join the school and swim with them. The few centimeters that separate the surface of the sea from the top

B

of the reef provide a habitat for colorful butterflyfish, who "graze" on young polyps of small *Acropora* corals that have colonized the area. Enjoy this sight from a distance, because the space is quite cramped and you could easily cause grave damage to this fragile and already mistreated ecosystem.

E – Small gray morays (Siderea grisea) can be found where the vertical barrier of the small walls of Far Garden meet the sandy floor.

E

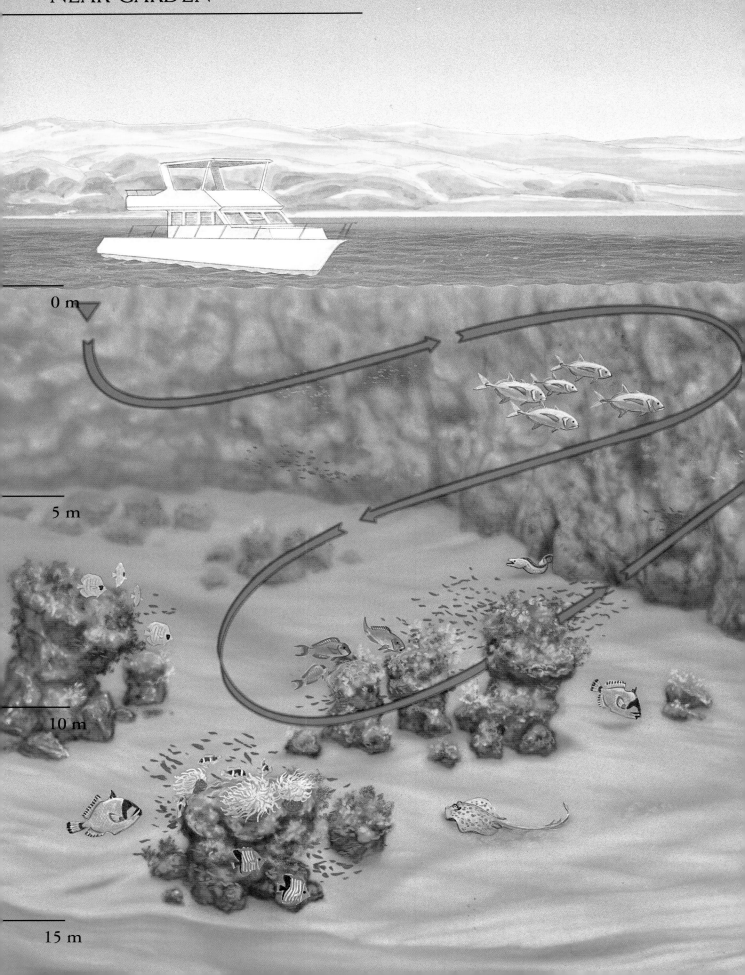

0 m

5 m

10 m

15 m

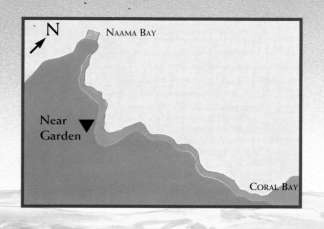

NAAMA BAY

Near Garden

CORAL BAY

N

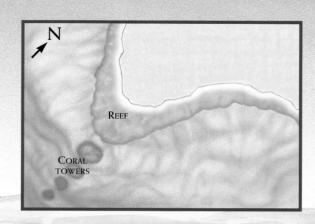

N

REEF

CORAL TOWERS

Departing from the new and always very crowded pier at Naama Bay, Near Garden is only about 10 minutes away, the first coral garden you'll find near the Naama Bay vacation area. Even though it's crowded with hotels and thousands of people, it's still one of the most interesting snorkeling sites. Its fortunate geographical position, always sheltered from the north winds, and the large variety of marine life, attract dozens of boats to the zone every day, loaded with enthusiastic coral explorers. Near Garden is also regularly visited by glass bottom boats that give people with no diving experience the chance to enjoy the multicolored, frenetic life of the coral reef. The area has two mooring lines attached to the bottom, where you can tie your boat. The surface reef drops in a vertical wall to a first shelf with a sandy bottom about 3-4 meters deep. The slope then descends gently to a depth of 20-25 meters, where it drops steeply into the deep blue sea.

Equipped with mask and flippers, you can start your excursion near the small wall that even a few centimeters below the surface has a myriad of cracks and recesses where schools of glassfish live, protected in shadow. They move in unison, creating fantastic plays of light with the sunshine that penetrates the surface cracks. Numerous parrotfish swim among the hard coral formations that decorate the wall. Occasionally they bite the coral to remove the layer of algae that covers it, leaving deep furrows in the substratum. Butterflyfish in a thousand colors move in pairs in a continuous search for food, while pairs of sedentary masked butterflyfish (*Chaetodon semilarvatus*) float immobile in the shadows, guarding their feeding territory. If you move from the wall and swim toward the open sea, you'll find

numerous coral pinnacles on the sandy shelf, covered with delicately colored alcyonarians and sea anemones (*Heteractis magnifica*). Clownfish (*Amphiprion bicinctus*) swim among its stinging tentacles, always ready to defend their small world from possible intrusion. The summit of these small coral towers is the undisputed reign of the anthias (*Pseudanthias squamipinnis*), who with their red purple color create fantastic chromatic contrasts with the thousand colors of the alcyonarians. Various *Pterois volitans* and radiata live sheltered in the small cavities, awaiting dark for their nocturnal hunting. Red soldierfish (*Myripristis murdjan*), who live in large groups of dozens of individuals, sometimes come out from their hiding places among the cracks. The head of a gray moray (*Siderea grisea*) peeps out from the base of the wall. This is the most common moray in the Red Sea, and it can also be found at very shallow depths. Its gray-yellow color scattered with small black spots on the head makes it easily visible even from the surface. Anyone with a trained eye may also see a crocodile fish (*Papilloculiceps longiceps*)

camouflaged on the sandy bottom.

Hidden by a thin layer of sand, the bluespotted ribbontail ray (*Taeniura lymma*) spends its days waiting for dark or high tide to scour the water's edge in search of its typical prey, mollusks and small crustaceans. The bluefin trevallies (*Caranx melampygus*) swim

quickly not far from the wall of the reef, always on the hunt. Sometimes they gather in very large schools of dozens of fish. It's always exciting to watch these silvery arrows passing by. During the full moon, it's common to see nests of titan triggerfish (*Balistoides viridescens*). Reproducing couples dig a hollow in the detrital floor, and after the female lays the eggs, both are extraordinarily aggressive in defending their territory. It really is amazing to watch these robust triggerfish continuously darting out at any fish that ventures near the area. Don't get too close, as they won't hesitate to attack a human far larger than they are, with extremely painful results for us.

A – In the Red Sea, the tides uncover wide areas of coral. Avoid walking on the semi-emerged reef, because you may step on a stonefish.

B – These corals appear to have been arranged by an expert landscape architect. Different species, for example gorgonians and alcyonarians, often live together on the same support.

C – A Pterois rests on the top of a stony coral colony.

D – The hawkfish (Paracirrhites forsteri) *can remain immobile for hours as it waits for a thoughtless prey.*

E – At night, trevallies (Caranx sexfasciatus) *are more active hunters. Before sunset, they gather in dense swarms and begin to patrol the reef in search of prey.*

RAS UMM SID

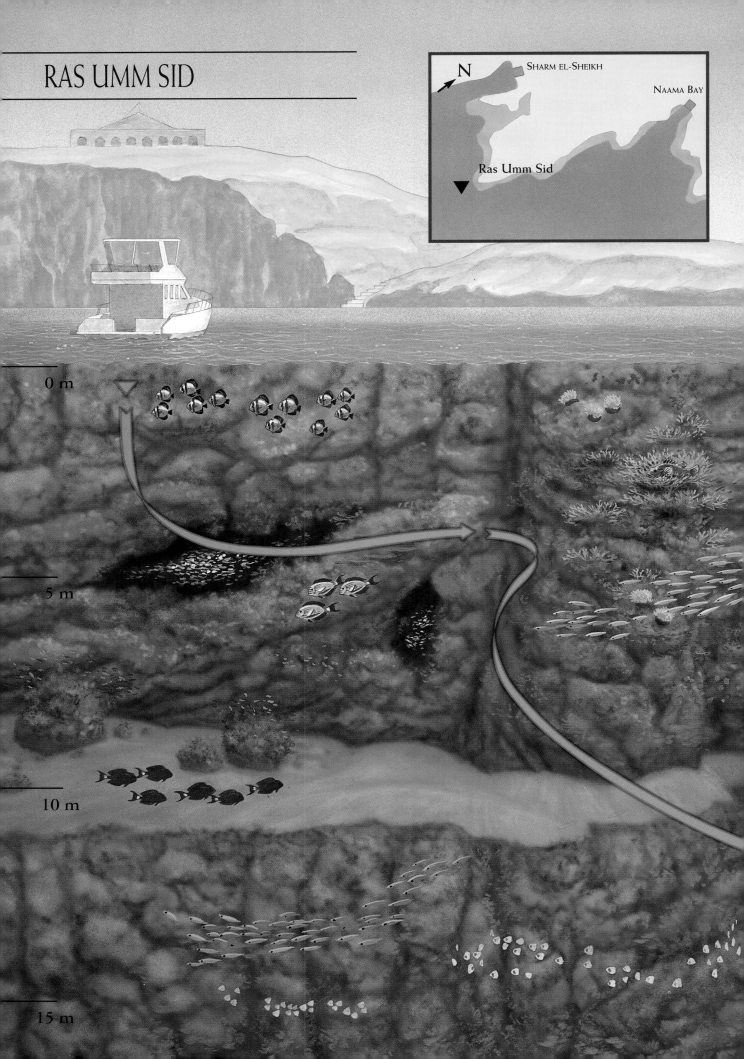

N

Sharm el-Sheikh

Naama Bay

Ras Umm Sid

0 m

5 m

10 m

15 m

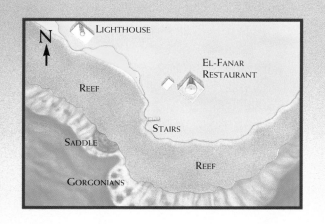

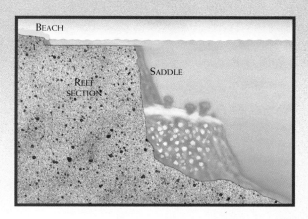

B

interesting part is the surface, as the reef is broken by deep cracks that offer shelter to swarms of glassfish (*Parapriacanthus guentheri*). In particular, visit the cave at about 5 meters deep. The spectacle offered by the sunlight striking these silvery fish is truly exciting. Large scorpion fish (*Scorpaenopsis oxycephala*) are quite common on the top of the reef, but be very careful, because they are extremely mimetic when lying immobile on the corals and look more like a rock than a fish. Surgeonfish (*Zebrasoma desjardini*) are quite common near anchorage areas. They move continuously from the wall to the anchored boats, where they graze on the encrusting algae that grow on the keels of the boats. Often during the summer months, large schools of batfish (*Platax orbicularis*) can be seen grazing under the boats tied to the mooring lines; it almost seems as if they intentionally try to stay in the shadow of the boats. They move slowly and elegantly, and with their streamlined form can even remain immobile

Sailing about 20 minutes north of the port of Sharm el-Mina, you'll come to one of the loveliest areas around Sharm el-Sheikh: the Ras Umm Sid promontory, surmounted by the lighthouse of the same name. You can also reach the area by land, following the road that leads to El-Fanar, a noted restaurant where

C

Fernando serves tasty Italian specialties. Right after it, you'll find a metal ladder to help you climb into the water. The surface reef stretches out about ten meters before it comes to the drop-off. It's highly inadvisable to walk out onto the corals: dozens of people who failed to follow this precaution have had personal experience with the Sharm hospital! The bay is traversed by a long, crowded beach equipped with lounge chairs and umbrellas, but if you go to the north end of the bay, it's absolutely peaceful. This is where you'll find the two anchoring *shamandura*. The outer one is better because it will broaden your field of action. The wall descends vertically to a depth of 25 meters, but the most

A – Below the boats moored at the shamandura, *dense schools of batfish (Platax orbicularis) often gather. During the summer months, this phenomenon is more frequent.*

B – The Ras Umm Sid lighthouse warns boats of the promontory that thrusts out into the open sea. It is advisable to explore the area near the northern tip for its greatest wealth of marine life.

C, D – The wall of Ras Umm Sid is famous for its forest of gorgonians, which begins just a few meters from the surface and ends in the deep blue depths. Gorgonians in this area are extremely large and numerous.

E – The coral pinnacles that reach the surface are ideal subjects for anyone looking for a glimpse into this frenetic world. Snorkeling allows us to enjoy the beauties of the sea.

D

E

A

A - A spectacular hunting scene. A Pterois immobile in the water sets a trap for a group of red anthias. Hovering against the current, the predator waits for a small fish to be pushed by the water and carried within striking distance.

B – The small inhabitants of the reef seek shelter in the tangle of corals whenever they feel threatened. A damselfish (Amblyglyphidodon leucogaster) hides among the branches of a red gorgonian.

B

Sharm el-Sheikh

C

D

E

against the current. The excursion proceeds toward the point of the promontory, keeping the reef to the left. An interesting ecosystem to observe is the branched Acropora and its small inhabitants, the chromis (Chromis viridis). As soon as they sense danger, these small fish take refuge among the tangled branches of coral, but they seem to be dancing rather than taking flight. Small schools of dentex (Lutjanus bohar) continuously patrol the area in search of prey, and often camouflage themselves among the large schools of fusiliers (Caesio suevica) that swim tirelessly in their constant search for zooplankton. The wall is bright with a thousand colors of the soft corals that thrive in this area due to the current that carries in nutrients, and colorful sea anemones with rounded tentacles offer shelter to delightful clownfish (Amphiprion bicinctus), with whom they live symbiotically throughout their lives. The truly unique spectacle that Ras Umm Sid offers is the forest of gorgonians hanging in clusters down to 35 meters deep. This waterfall of delicate lacework hosts a large variety of marine life, including the hawkfish (Oxycirrhites typus), skillfully camouflaged among its branches as it awaits careless victims who venture too close. Pterois volitans dance in the water with their feathery pectoral fins, and butterflyfish feast on the polyps of the soft corals they find so tasty. The gorgonians signal the outer limit of the point, so once you get this far, you should look out into the open sea, as it's almost always possible to see a school of young barracudas darting rapidly in the current. They should remind you that it's time to turn back to the boat, lest the slight current running north from this point makes your return difficult.

0 m

5 m

10 m

15 m

N

Sharm el-Sheikh

Sharm el-Maya

Naama Bay

▼ Temple

N

BEACH

BUILDINGS

REEF

A – Glassfish (Parapriacanthus guentheri) reflect the sunlight in golden flashes. At night, these tiny creatures disperse along the reef to hunt. Their disproportionately large eyes are a sign of their nocturnal habits.

B – A red coral grouper (Cephalopholis miniata) with its mouth open. Quite probably a cleaner wrasse is intent on removing remains of food and parasites from its gills.

Temple is one of the easiest areas to reach from the harbor of Sharm el-Mina. In fact, in just a fifteen minute sail north, you'll come to the bay across from the most crowded beach in all of Sharm. It's one of the most popular places with diving neophytes, because it forms a natural swimming pool off the beach, where the white sand of the bottom creates extremely lovely reflections of the strong sunlight. This section of the sea is the destination of numerous glass-bottom boats that allow even those who don't dive the chance to enjoy the many beauties that the underwater world offers. Various anchorage points allow the boats to moor in the central portion of the gulf, so you'll have quite a bit of territory to explore. The most interesting area surrounds the approximately ten coral towers that rise from the sandy floor 10 meters deep, giving Temple its name. The coral pinnacles come almost to the surface and form a sort of

B

C

D

colonnade. The most imposing of these formations almost rises out of the water and is the only one that allows snorkelers to closely explore the area. Unfortunately, Temple is a popular place for night dives, and the hundreds of scuba divers who explore the stony coral towers every week have gradually destroyed these enormous coral formations. Fortunately, the upper portion of these structures is less damaged, and the life of the reef still offers exciting sights to anyone armed with a mask and flippers who wants to explore the frenetic life of the reef from the surface. Thus, you should focus your attention on the "roofs" covered in brilliant violet alcyonarians, surrounded by clouds of purple anthias moving jerkily to catch plankton carried by the current. Stony coral formations known as fire coral grow on the top. Be very careful not to brush

C – Raccoon butterflyfish (Caethon semilarvatus) are quite curious, and if approached cautiously will not retreat, but remain to watch you inquisitively.

D – Fire coral (Millepora dichotoma) needs light to spread. For this reason, hydrozoans are more common in surface waters of tropical seas.

A

E

F

E – The image shows a female Pseudantias squamipinnis. *When the male of the harem dies, the dominant female changes sex and takes his place. The species is diurnal and takes refuge among the corals at night.*

F – The water is so clear across from the beach at Temple that from the water's surface you can see down to the sandy floor, where the sea bed is dotted with coral mushrooms populated by marine life.

against the small apical branches of this hydrozoan, because they sting and could cause painful burns.

Regular visitors to Temple include humphead wrasses (*Cheilinus undulatus*) who curiously but warily approach, ready to flee at the first hint of danger. Despite the fact that they can become quite

large, they're completely harmless, and even though you may be a bit intimidated by their size, it's quite safe to approach them. You can see numerous red coral groupers (*Cephalopholis miniata*) sheltered in shaded areas as they lie in ambush for small fish, especially anthias, who carelessly enter their territory. These voracious predators live in harems comprised of a male and numerous females.

Also look at the area near the coastline, where the reef drops vertically from the surface to the sandy floor about 3-4 meters deep. Not many people come here, so you can see little schools of fish swimming tranquilly without being disturbed by the usual traffic of

A – Clownfish (Amphiprion bicinctus) takes shelter among the tentacles of a sea anemone, to whose poison it is immune.

B – The anemone crab (Neopetrolisthes ohshimai) lives in the shelter of the actinia, with which it has a symbitic relationship. The former cleans the latter of parasites and particles of food that have escaped its mouth.

C – The yellowedge lyretail (Variola louti) can commonly be seen swimming, but is difficult to approach.

A

B

swimmers. Small blue and yellow fusiliers (Caesio suevica) live in this habitat, floating motionless in dense groups near the surface, along with pairs of masked butterflyfish (Chaetodon semilarvatus) who share the twilight of the cracks with groups of blackspotted

sweetlips (Plectorhynchus gaterinus), bright yellow with black spots. It's not uncommon to see large star pufferfish (Arothron stellatus) on the sea bed, resting on the sand and looking for all the world as if they were napping. These comical-looking reef inhabitants, easily

C

E

recognizable by their oval shape and gray color with small black spots, can become quite large, up to a meter in length. The shallow waters and bright sunlight allow algae to grow abundantly, attracting many longnose unicorn tangs (Naso brevirostris), an herbivorous species that's easily recognizable by the horn growing out past its eyes. As you explore the towers, never move out to the open sea, perhaps to follow a fish, because boats are constantly moving from the anchorage points.

D

D – Barracudas (Shyraena sp.) move in large groups from the open sea to the reef as they patrol their territory.

E – The giant pufferfish (Arothron stellatus) is one of the largest species in the Tetraodontidae family, and may reach 90 cm in length.

F – Blennies (Ecsenius midas) live in small cavities in the reef. From these safe shelters, they can control the entire surrounding territory.

MARSA BAREIKA

0 m

5 m

10 m

SINAI

N

SHARM EL-SHEIKH

Marsa Bareika

THE QUAY

RAS MOHAMMED

Pointing the prow of your boat south of the port of Sharm el-Mina, in about an hour you'll reach Marsa Bareika, a deep inlet that is part of the Ras Mohammed marine park district. The rock desert in this area softens and slopes toward the sea in fine sand dunes, transforming into a very long beach. It's a very interesting area from the naturalistic perspective not only because of the sea floor, but also because this is a resting place for

A – The small lemon goby (Gobiodon citrinus) lives among the branches of Acropora corals.

B – The Eretmochelis imbricata turtle is the most frequent species in the Red Sea.

C – Among the tenctacles of anemones clownfish (Amphiprion bicinctus) and domino damselfish (Dascillus trimaculatus) find shelter.

D – The lizardfish (Synodus variegatus) owes its name to its habit of keeping its head raised. Due to its strong pectoral fins, it can easily 'walk' on the floor of the sea.

E – Gobies from the species Valenciennea puellaris live in tunnel-

shaped dens that they dig in the detrital bed by moving the sand with their mouths.

F – The crocodile fish (Cociella crocodila), a member of the Scorpaeniformes order, is a typical resident of sandy and detrital beds, where

they bury themselves in order to surprise and capture their prey.

G – This porcupine fish (Diodon histrix) can be recognized by the spines that cover its body. It can raise the spines for defense purposes when it senses danger.

A

B

C

many birds during their great migrations from Europe to Africa. In fact, in late summer you can see hundreds of storks resting on the beach before taking up the long voyage to their final destination. The bay is quite deep, and thus well sheltered, and sea conditions are always excellent for snorkeling. The sea floor is sandy and slopes gently to a depth of 20-25 meters, then drops in a vertical wall. The plateau is scattered with small rocky

formations that are home to a wealth of different species. Take your time with this excursion, because every coral mushroom is an explosion of life and should be examined very carefully. The sea is also very calm here, with exceptional visibility, so you can spend a long time in the water. The shallow floor and bright sunlight create shining reflections on the sand, where you can see numerous flattened-looking crocodile fish

with large mouths that resemble the reptile that gives them their name. On the detrital areas, which seem lifeless, you'll actually find extraordinary life forms that are invisible at first glance. There are dozens of pipefish (Corythoichthys schultzi), their thin, elongated bodies moving sinuously on the floor in search of the small crustaceans on which they feed, catching and swallowing them with their elongated mouths that act as a

D

E

reef inhabitant should be closely watched, because it's one of the oddest creatures of the coral kingdom. It's not uncommon to find a large *Arothron ispidus*, a member of the pufferfish family, lazily resting on the floor. This comical-looking fish is olive brown spattered with white spots. Avoid touching these peaceful creatures, because despite their rather awkward appearance, they have a quick reaction time and sharp teeth! In the winter and spring, the currents bring large quantities of plankton into Marsa Bareika, which inevitably attract microorganism filter feeders. In fact, it wouldn't be uncommon to meet up with a manta, its mouth wide open as it elegantly glides near the surface. Appearing suspended near the water's surface, you'll see groups of bigeye emperors (*Monotaxis grandoculis*), members of the *Letrinidae*

F

G

suction pump. There may also be a lizardfish (*Saurida gracilis*) half-buried in the sand, camouflaged and lying in wait for any small fish that carelessly comes too close to its mouth, armed with teeth that are visible even when its jaws are closed. The floor is scattered with holes, near which you can find Steinitz's gobies (*Amblyeleotris steinitzi*). This little fish, white with five dark diagonal bands on its sides, shares its den with an *Alpheus* shrimp in a

symbiotic relationship that is one of the most fascinating of the marine world. Just watch the entrance of the den for a few seconds and you'll see the little crustacean busily housecleaning, removing sand and small pebbles that it evidently wanted out of its dwelling. Watching carefully among the stony branches of the *Acropora*, you'll see dozens of brilliant yellow little lemon gobies (*Gobiodon citrinus*) with narrow azure stripes. This curious

family, silvery in color and sometimes over 40 centimeters long. When frightened, they rapidly grow darker in color. The long beach is one of the places sea turtles prefer to deposit their eggs. The hours before dusk are thus a good time to see females waiting for the right moment to climb to land and dig a hole in the sand, where they'll leave their precious cargo.

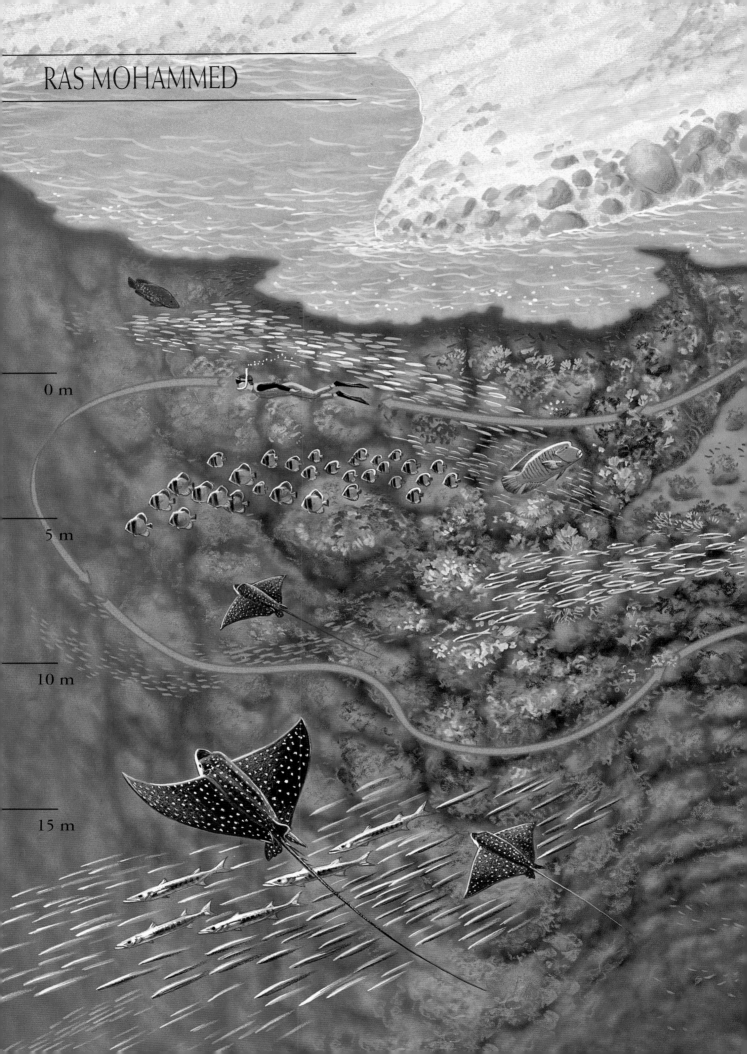

0 m

5 m

10 m

15 m

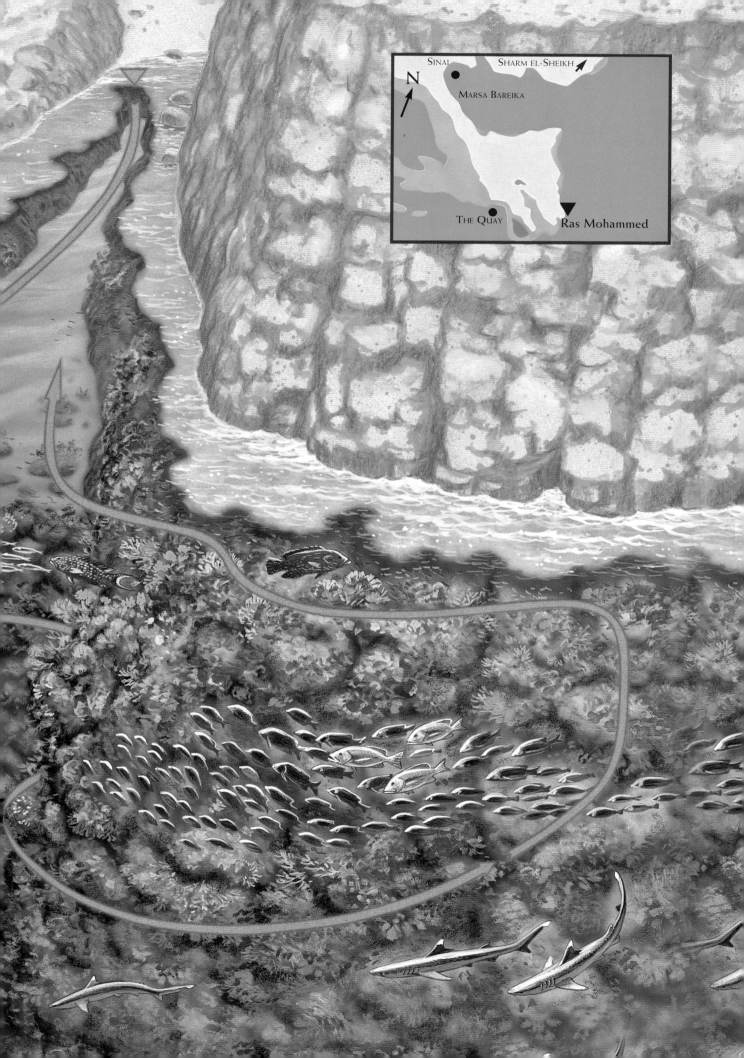

SINAI

SHARM EL-SHEIKH

MARSA BAREIKA

N

THE QUAY

Ras Mohammed

R as Mohammed is the extreme southern tip of the Sinai Peninsula. This area has been protected since 1983, and a Marine Park has been created to protect an ecosystem of extraordinary naturalistic importance. The National Park was expanded in 1989, and now the protected district covers an area 11,000 square kilometers in size. The point of departure for your excursion will be the beach below the rocky buttress known as Shark Observatory. Every day, local operators bring hundreds of people here on buses traveling the scenic road that leads from Sharm to Hidden Bay in a little over an hour. The best way to visit the park, which also includes a mangrove forest (*Avicennia marina*) is to hire a cab and get there early in the morning before hordes of bathers have invaded the place! Before you go into the water, it's absolutely vital to check for currents, a not uncommon event, and use extreme caution in your exploration. Enter the water at the little beach that interrupts reefs which drop vertically from the surface to the abyss. Avoid walking on the semi-emerged reef to reach other entry points. In addition to destroying hundreds

of years of work by reef building polyps, you also risk getting serious abrasions that almost always result in dangerous infections. Never forget that the coral reef is not an inanimate object – every structure that makes it up is a living animal! As soon as you immerse your head in the water, you'll see an explosion of life and color that you'll rarely find anywhere else on the now damaged Sharm coast. Great currents of water from the Gulf of Suez and the Gulf of Aqaba converge here, carrying in large quantities of plankton that create ideal conditions for the development of all the invertebrates that constitute the marvelous world of corals. Even in the first few meters, the size and colors of the alcyonarians and stony corals are absolutely extraordinary, true flowering bushes around which swim a myriad of multicolored fish. *Anthias*, omnipresent inhabitants of the coral reefs, seem larger and brighter than usual, their red-orange scales standing out in sharp contrast against the deep

blue sea. The vertical wall is extremely irregular, with spurs of rock jutting out toward the open sea, alternating with deep recesses from which hang trees of black coral. In the early morning it's not uncommon to see whitetip reef sharks (*Trianodon obesus*) patrolling the deeper regions. With a bit of

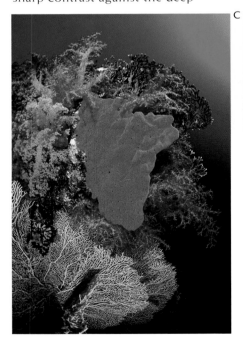

A – The buttresses of the arid Sinai mountains thrust into the sea, transforming into walls of rich marine life just below the surface.

B, C – Ras Mohammed has a unique variety of sea beds. Gorgonians, sponges and alcyonarians create truly spectacular masses of color.

D – Sharks, which were once more numerous in these waters, have now moved to areas less frequented by man.

E – Trevallies are a constant presence around the semi-emerged pinnacle at Shark Reef.

F – Snappers (Lutjanus bohar) gather along the vertical walls of the Ras Mohammed reefs, succumbing to the irresistible urge to reproduce.

luck, you may encounter elegant eagle rays swimming effortlessly against the current. Some large groupers who have abandoned their dens float near the surface, lying in wait for fusiliers moving about in large groups along the coral slope. As you swim across the surface, you'll invariably meet up with a humphead wrasse (*Cheilinus undulatus*), who curiously approaches snorkelers almost close enough to touch. The humphead wrasse is certainly one of the oddest-looking inhabitants of the tropical seas, with the characteristic hump on its forehead that gives it its name. During the summer months, the irresistible urge to reproduce attracts enormous concentrations of fish to this area. Massing together to form true living walls, they create a unique spectacle. Just under the surface you can see silvery masses of hundreds of batfish (*Platax teira*) that reflect the bright sunlight in glittering flashes. Farther down, dense groups of barracudas swim in circles until they begin to resemble a ball of metallic light. There are also trevallies (*Caranx sexfasciatus*), often swimming in pairs, with males and females sporting completely different colors, one gray and the other black. Green surgeonfish (*Naso*

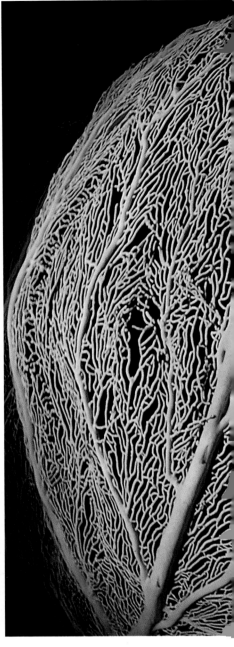

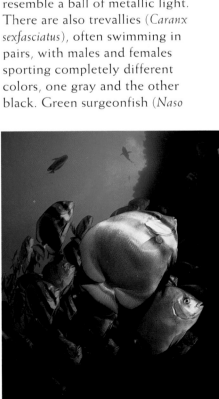

hexacanthus) float immobile in dense groups in the column of water, waiting for the current to bring them the zooplankton on which they feed. But the most spectacular sight of all is the wall of snappers (*Lutjanus bohar*) who gather in impressive schools like slow-moving walls. You can also explore the two outer reefs of Ras Mohammed, Shark Reef and Jolanda Reef, but only when there is absolutely no current, and only if you travel there by boat.

A – Platax *use the recesses of the wall for protection against the current. Their discoid form is not an ideal structure for swimming against the current.*

B – *A red coral grouper (Cephalopholis miniata) appears from a formation of soft corals that resembles a flowering bouquet.*

C – *The fans of this gorgonian offer shelter to a Pterois. The branches also hide small fish that make up its regular diet.*

D – *The image shows an alcyonarian set into the filigree of the gorgonianis branches. The position the soft coral has chosen, right in the current, allows more luxuriant growth due to the greater abundance of nourishment.*

E – *In the winter, mantas (Manta birostris) seek the coast to be cared for by industrious cleaner wrasses. Mantas lead a pelagic life and follow the flows of plankton as they swim in the open sea.*

E   F

F — Sea turtles abandon the sea bed to come to the surface to breathe. These reptiles pass their entire lives in oceanic meadows and only come on land to reproduce.

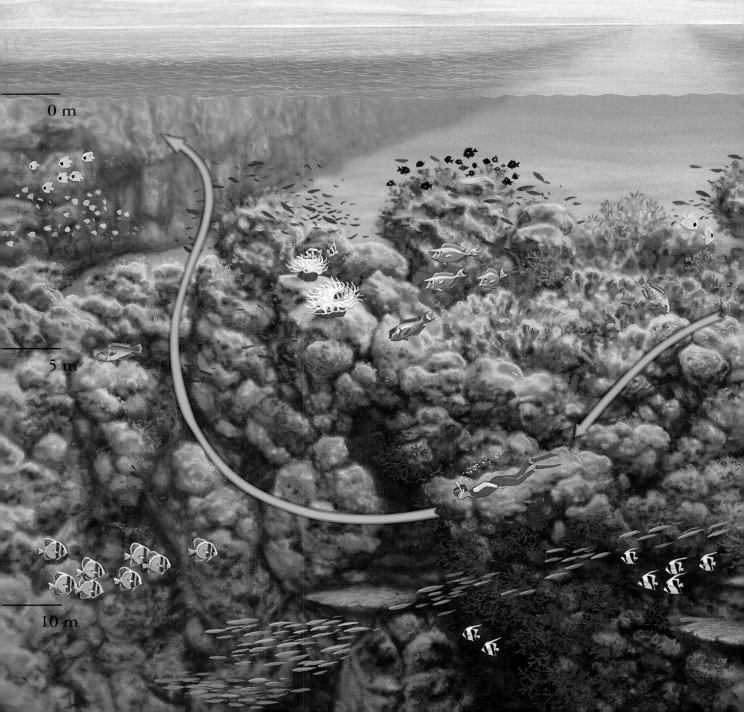

0 m

5 m

10 m

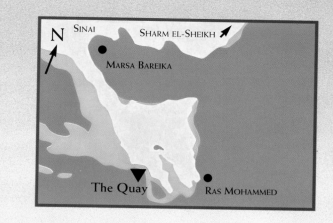

Leaving the harbor of Sharm el-Mina, head south, and once you reach the promontory of Ras Mohammed, continue to sail along the coastline to just beyond the lighthouse that marks the southernmost point of the Sinai Peninsula. You'll enter a deep inlet known as the Quay. On the northern side of the gulf there are

A – Sea conditions within the gulf of Quay are always excellent, and snorkeling is possible any time during the year.

B – The emperor angelfish (Pomacanthus imperator) can often be seen swimming near the reef, where it seeks out the sponges and algae on which it feeds. If it senses danger, it emits clicking sounds.

C – A giant moray (Gymnothorax javanicus) is swimming out of its den.

D, E – Sandy sea beds are the reign of large rayfish. A rare drab stingray (Hypolophus sephen) can easily be identified by the long tail ending in a plume.

various shamandura, or mooring lines, and sea conditions here are always excellent for snorkeling. On days when the wind is strong, a rather common occurrence, divers bring their boats here to take shelter from the rough sea between dives. The boat is anchored rather close to the reef, and after a brief swim, you'll come to the coral wall, which runs vertically from the surface to about twenty meters deep. Some portions of the wall are broken by passageways that allow you to reach the beach that fringes the whole gulf. In the late summer, thousands of storks stop over here during their seasonal migrations. The reef near

the surface is adorned by thick bushes of soft corals, such as Alcyonaria. Hundreds of red anthias, perhaps the most numerous inhabitants of the coral reef, swim around them as if dancing. Stony corals are also well represented by Acropora, with their fantastic shape like large umbrellas, and other stony

corals like Porites, which have a smooth, velvety-looking surface when examined closely. Hydrozoans like Millepora or fire corals deserve a whole separate discussion. If you touch them, they'll cause painful burns. When in doubt, follow the snorkeler's most important rule: never touch anything if you want to

D

E

F – Exploring the coral wall often reveals dense clusters of alcyonarians and gorgonians that undulate to the rhythm of the surf.

bicinctus), who will attack and drive off anyone who invades their territory. Various types and sizes of butterflyfish move in pairs, continuously biting at the coral with their pointed snouts to pull off the polyps on which they feed. Even unicornfish (*Naso unicornis*) are usually present in small groups swimming near the wall.

Exploring the shallow, sandy floor that leads to the beach, you'll see numerous damselfish gobies and Steinitz gobies outside their dens dug in the sand. These fish are quite timid, and all it takes is a brusque movement or a shift in the water to make them disappear inside their tunnels. It's not uncommon to see a batfish (*Platax teira*) swim by. These fish have a characteristic flattened, discoid, silvery body, and gather together in the summer for reproduction in schools of hundreds of individuals.

F

end your vacation in good health! Near a recess in the wall is a spectacular formation of brilliant red chickenfoot sponges that looks like a cascade of intertwining vermilion branches. Groups of fusiliers (*Caesio suevicus*) pass by continuously in the open water, followed by their mortal enemies, the swift trevallies.

For small fish, staying in a compact school is a defense strategy, as predators cannot focus their attack on a specific individual when it's in a mass of constantly moving companions. Delicate sea anemones have colonized several small terraces, joined by their amusing tenants, the clownfish (*Amphiprion*

EL-GOUNA

Strait of Gobal

E – The image shows a redtooth triggerfish (Odonus niger) exploring the reef.

F – One of the attractions of Gota Abu Nuhas is the large schools of yellowfin goatfish that gather in the recesses of the reef.

GOBAL ISLAND

TAWILA ISLAND

▲ Gota Abu Nuhas

SHADWAN ISLAND

Shaab el-Erg ▼

El-Bayud Reef ▲

Poseidon ▲

El-Gouna ●

Ras Abu Kalawa ▼

A – The architectural solutions used to build the El-Gouna tourist facility are based on respect for the environment and Arabic styles and traditions. The maze of canals and bridges that cross them make them look like a little oriental Venice.

B – Numerous islets and stony coral reefs rise from the deep sea off the coast of El-Gouna, where coral life explodes in all its beauty.

C – The photo shows a batfish (Platax teira) swimming peacefully.

D - Shaab el-Erg, a crescent-shaped reef also known as Dolphin Reef, is one of the areas where you can find these very friendly mammals.

El-Gouna is the latest star of Egyptian tourism. Located 22 kilometers north of the Hurghada airport at the foot of rugged mountains overlooking the crystalline waters of the Red Sea, the El-Gouna vacation area is beyond doubt one of the most exclusive in the entire region. Built on an archipelago of little islands connected by bridges suspended over turquoise lagoons, the El-Gouna facilities extend over a surface area of over 10 million square meters of virgin territory, with

B

C

kilometers of sandy beaches that are still completely unspoiled. The vacation area is completely self-sufficient, and in addition to about ten first class hotels, it includes public facilities with restaurants, discotheques, pubs, fitness centers, shopping centers, an 18-hole golf course, and of course, diving centers for anyone interested in underwater excursions. El-Gouna's development

was carefully planned, with a high priority for safeguarding the beauty of the area as well as ensuring fully functional environmental tourism. The environment has been fully protected as the area has developed, so that El-Gouna has become known as the "the most environmentally protected vacation area in Egypt." From the Marine Center, you can quickly reach secluded reefs with pristine floors. like El-Erg and Abu Kalawa, where you can spend a relaxing day snorkeling and exploring the fantastic coral gardens and their frenetic life. Off the coast, you'll find islands rising from the depths of the Red Sea, fringed by splendid white sand beaches. Some of these include the two Gobal Islands, Tawila Island, where you can get off your boat for a pleasant walk along the beach, or the two Siyul Islands. The lagoons with their detrital floors around the islands should also be explored with mask and flippers. At first glance, these sea floors may seem void of life, but they actually have extremely interesting structures and life forms. Between the islands and the mainland you'll find long, semi-emerged coral reefs that are true explosions of movement and color. In the upper areas of the reef, which are more exposed to sunlight, reef building polyps find ideal conditions

D

E

F

for developing and building skeletons in extraordinary forms and sizes. When weather conditions are ideal, you can explore the wreck of a boat that sank on the reef at Abu Nuhas in the early 1980s. The remains of the hull are visible from the surface and have been completely colonized by corals and fish who find refuge and nourishment among the contorted wreckage, now covered with sponges and stony corals. El-Gouna offers something special and different from other areas on the Egyptian coast: secluded beaches and exclusive hotels, lively night life and still pristine sea floors that hold truly exciting discoveries.

0 m

6 m

12 m

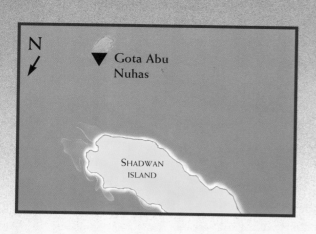

N

▼ Gota Abu
   Nuhas

SHADWAN
ISLAND

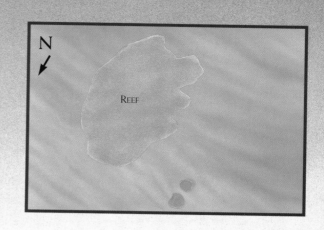

N

REEF

Your destination lies about an hour and a half away by boat from El-Gouna and is located north of the large island of Shadwan, not far from the Shaab Abu Nuhas reef, famous among divers because the floors of its north wall hold three of the most spectacular shipwrecks in the entire Red Sea. The trip will often be interrupted by the usual schools of dolphins, and the boat will stop a few minutes to give snorkelers a chance for a close encounter with one of these fascinating sea creatures. Once you reach the *gota*, you will see that it's almost circular in shape, with the exposed portion to the east broken by numerous deep cracks that run from the surface down the entire wall of the reef to the bottom, almost like wide vertical canyons.

Secure the boat to a mooring buoy on the southeast side of the coral formation, over a sandy bottom about 8-10 meters deep. Once you

enter the water, head north, keeping the walls to your left. The upper portion of the reef is a true explosion of hard corals in a thousand forms and colors. You'll also find broad tables of *Acropora* with their unmistakable umbrella shape, beneath which groups of bannerfish (*Heniochus intermedius*) turn curiously as you pass, following you with their eyes. There are dense groups of fire corals with the omnipresent anthias circling around them. Sheltered in the cracks, squirrelfish (*Sargocentron diadema*) wait for dusk, when they come out in search of food. At the second canyon from the south, near the surface, there is usually a dense

school of small barracudas, who if cautiously approached can be observed very close up. If you push them too far toward the semi-emerged part of the reef, they'll slip away like a silvery river, creating metallic reflections under the sunlight.

Other permanent inhabitants of Gota Abu Nuhas are the yellowfin goatfish (*Mulloides vanicolensis*), who defend themselves by forming dense groups, disorienting predators with their large, continuously moving mass. When you dive in, you'll invade the compact group of goatfish, which will disperse in a thousand directions, only to regroup

E

F

F – A beautiful hawkfish (Paracirrhites forsteri) appears to be resting among the branches of a fire *coral. It is actually patiently waiting for a careless fish to swim into its hunting territory, to be fallen upon in a lightning strike.*

A

B

C

D – The longnose hawkfish (Oxycirrhites typus) is camouflaged among the gorgonians.

E – A rare formation of Ellisella whip coral extends its thread-like colonies toward the open sea.

F – A school of small yellowtail barracudas (Sphyraena flavicauda) hovers near the surface during the daylight hours. When night comes, the group disperses and each individual hunts alone.

A – Dense schools of yellowfin goatfish (Mulloides vanicolensis) move en masse in the shallower portion of the reef. Below are Porites stony coral formations.

B – The emperor angelfish (Pomacanthus imperator), easily recognizable by its showy colors, lives a solitary life within a well-defined territory.

C – The nudibranch (Nembrotha megalocera), an endemic species in the Red Sea, usually crawls on the sea floor, but if it senses danger, it can also swim in the open water.

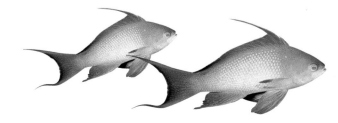

When you see one of these fish guarding a hollow on the detrital bottom, keep away.

Sohal surgeonfish (*Acanthurus sohal*) swim expertly just below the surface, their ventral portions brushing the corals as they sail through the surf.

In the afternoon you're likely to see several *Pterois* moving elegantly in the open water, allowing their soft fins to float like feathers in hopes that some small fish will lower its guard for a moment, to be fallen upon in a lightning attack almost invisible to the naked eye. With a little patience, you may witness one of the coral reef's most spectacular and dramatic moments.

Be careful not to move too far north, because during some times of

when you return to the surface.

The brain corals show unmistakable signs of the sharp beak of the parrotfish, large numbers of which circle at shallow depths, munching the corals to feed on the algae that live in symbiosis

with their polyps.

Some solitary titan triggerfish (*Balistoides viridescens*) can be seen on the sandy bottom at the base of the *gota*. Swimming vertically with their mouths to the floor, they blow jets of water onto the bottom to move detritus and find the mollusks and crustaceans that make up their normal diet. Their strong teeth can crush even the hardest shell.

This peaceful reef inhabitant transforms into a potential danger to anyone who approaches its nest while it is depositing its eggs, usually during the full moon.

the day a slight current could carry you far from the boat, making it extremely difficult to get back on board. You should have no problems if you stay on the southeast side of the hard coral formation.

Not many snorkelers visit the Gota Abu Nuhas reef, so the whole reef area you can explore is completely intact. Be careful not to come too close to the corals, especially at very shallow depths. Just one careless move will instantly destroy cathedrals that the coral polyps took dozens of years to create.

SHAAB EL-ERG

0 m

5 m

10 m

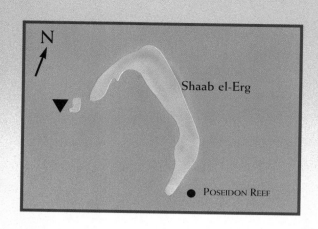

Shaab el-Erg

Poseidon Reef

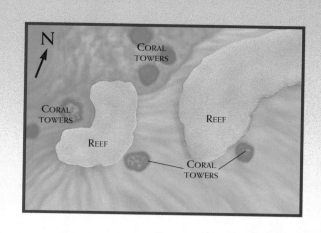

CORAL TOWERS

CORAL TOWERS

REEF

REEF

CORAL TOWERS

A – Spectacular clusters of stony coral from the genus *Acropora* grow in countless forms. They develop as they seek to expose as much surface area as possible to the sun and current.

B – One of the most fascinating spectacles that can be seen from the surface is the explosion of colors created by the Alcyonaria, extraordinary quantities of which have colonized the walls of this reef. A colorful parrotfish can be seen swimming among the anthias.

C – Trevallies (Carangoides bajad) on the hunt. These predators live in small groups and usually swim very close to the sea floor, taking advantage of protrusions to hide and then surprise schools of small fish.

Leaving the Miramar marina of El-Gouna and sailing about an hour east, you'll come to the reef group known as Shaab el-Erg. The long coral formation has the characteristic shape of a horseshoe open to the southwest where a *gota* (a semi-emerging coral formation more or less circular in shape) juts out from the main reef. Numerous pinnacles rise from the sandy bottom of the lagoon, sometimes all the way to the surface. On the southern and northern ends of the reef are two lighthouses that signal the presence of this insidious natural obstacle to sailing: at low tide, numerous coral blocks can be seen above the surface!

Sea conditions are usually excellent due to the shelter provided by the long reef, and the currents create no problems for any snorkeler who wants to observes the extraordinary spectacle that this area offers. Your boat can be moored at one of the numerous *shamandura* found along the south side of the reef. Try to secure it to one of the buoys near the *gota*, as this is one of the most interesting areas to explore.

The sandy bottom below the keel of the boat varies in depth between 6 and 10 meters. At this point, the coral reef rises in a nearly vertical wall to just a few centimeters from the surface. Begin exploring counterclockwise, keeping the reef to your left. You'll immediately be surrounded by a multitude of sergeant majors (*Abudefduf sexatilis*), their bodies an unmistakable yellow color with black vertical bands, who will accompany you curiously for the

D – A silvery mass of glassfish (Parapriacanthus guentheri) lives in this shadowy crevice. During the day, these little fish, glinting with golden light, prefer the more sheltered, safer areas of the coral reef.

E

F

E – Sergeant majors (Abudefduf vaigiensis) live in large schools just below the surface of the sea not far from the reef, and can easily be approached by snorkelers.

F – A bluespotted stingray (Taeniura lymma) uses its mouth to dredge detritus from the sea bed, in search of the worms and shrimp on which it feeds. These stingrays, with their sedentary habits, come out at night and during hightides.

A

B

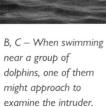

A – Dolphins are sometimes suspicious. To avoid frightening them, you should make no abrupt moves. C

B, C – When swimming near a group of dolphins, one of them might approach to examine the intruder.

The first to venture close are males responsible for the safety of the group.

D – Mantas (Manta birostris) come near the reef when they need to have parasites removed.

entire dive. The shallower part of the reef offers a marvelous seascape of perfectly intact hard coral formations surrounded by swarms of bright purple anthias. Near the surface, compact formations of cornetfish (*Fistularia commersonii*) float immobile, mimicking the surrounding environment in order to ambush their prey. Near the channel that separates the *gota* from the rest of the reef, the wall is embellished with small gorgonians and tufts of soft corals (*Alcyonaria*)

in delicate pastel colors. On the west side of the hard coral base, at a depth of 2 to 4 meters, the wall is broken by several cracks, within which platoons of glassfish (*Parapriacanthus guentheri*) dart. All around are parrotfish and butterflyfish, ceaselessly searching for food. On the sandy bottom you can see characteristic bluespotted ribbontail rays (*Taeniura lymma*). Shaab el-Erg is nevertheless famous for the community of dolphins that has

chosen this tranquil lagoon for its home. You can swim for hours among dozens of these marvelous marine mammals, who will curiously take turns coming so close that you can almost touch them. It's hard to describe this almost breathtaking experience. Meeting dolphins in the open sea is certainly an uncommon event, and you'll be fascinated by the elegant, seemingly effortless underwater maneuvers and leaps into the air of these extraordinary swimmers.

One precaution: if you touch the delicate skin of the dolphins, be very careful not to scratch their silky epidermis with any rings or watches, as this could cause infection. In the winter months, other giants of the sea frequent the waters around Shaab el-Erg. The abundant plankton in this zone lures manta rays, which are common near the surface, elegantly gliding as they filter the nutrient-rich water. As you observe the bottom and the teeming life that populates it, avoid coming too close to the reef with your fins, which could damage it irreparably. Always remember this fundamental rule: a coral touched is a coral killed!

E – Bottlenose dolphins usually live in groups: the separate pods of females and adult males gather together only during the mating season.

F – Dolphins are able swimmers and can exceed a speed of 20 knots. They feed on a large variety of prey, such as gray mullets, anchovies, sardines, mackerel, and squid.

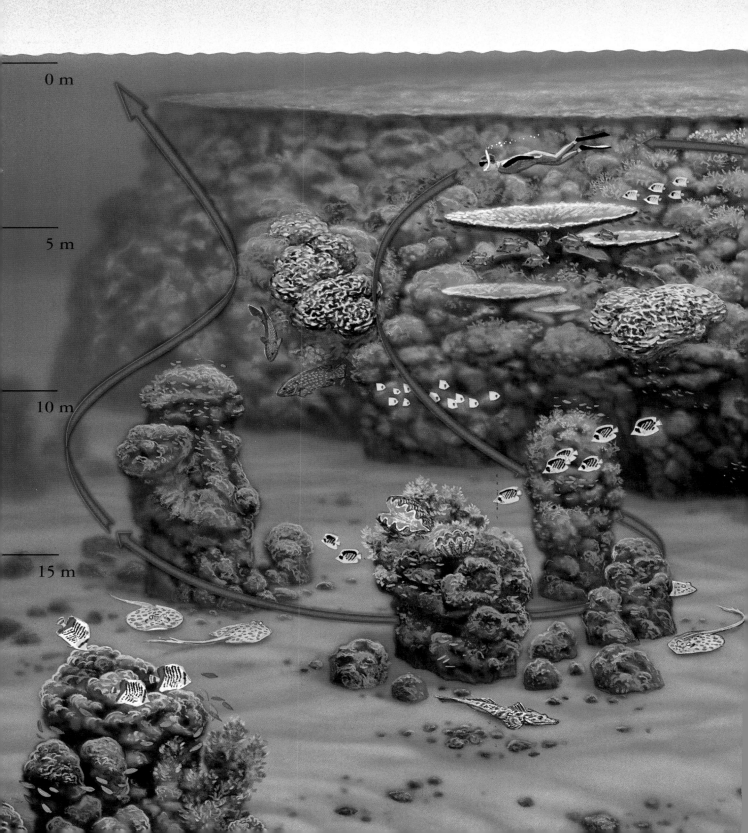

POSEIDON REEF

0 m

5 m

10 m

15 m

SHAAB EL-ERG

Poseidon Reef

N

A

Not far from the southwest side of the Shaab el-Erg coral group is an elongated hard coral formation that rises to about one meter from the surface. The walls of the reef descend perpendicular to the sandy bottom to a depth of about 10-12 meters. Near the northwest side, you'll see numerous blocks of coral teeming with life, and on the south side, about 5 meters away from the main wall, is a satellite reef similar to a stubby tower rising toward the surface. You reach the area by sailing about one hour east from El-Gouna. On the south side of Poseidon Reef are several mooring buoys where you can anchor your boat. The excursion can begin by circumnavigating the isolated block and then approaching the wall and paddling northward, keeping it to your right. Favored by nutrient-rich, limpid, warm waters, corals grow here in all their beauty, creating fantastical and apparently chaotic structures that actually follow quite precise schemes. Imposing agglomerates of fire coral (*Millepora dichotoma*) interweave with their branches to form true bushes. There are small *Acropora* corals with delicate pink tips, and spectacular groups of hard *Turbinaria mesenterina* corals that look like bunches of piled greenish-yellow leaves.

The spaces that corals have not covered contain numerous giant clams, set like precious stones in vivid colors running from yellow to green and blue to brown, each one with different shades. These delicate bivalve mollusks, which can reach over a meter in length and weigh up to 250 kg, have mantles that take their colors from the presence of large quantities of zooxanthellae, single-celled algae that live in symbiosis with all coral formations. The growth and thus the good health of the zooxanthellae depends on the quantity of light that reaches them. The Red Sea, whose extraordinarily transparent water allows sunlight to reach great depths, offers these symbiotic algae perfect conditions for growth. The fantastic hard coral clusters of the reef along the

D

E

B

C

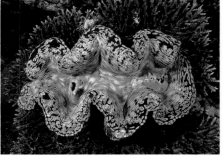

A – The waters of the Red Sea are so transparent that you can admire underwater life even from the surface.

B – The raccoon butterflyfish (Chaetodon fasciatus) lives a solitary life in the flat areas of the reef. It's easily identified by the black mask around the eye area.

C – A giant clam has grown among the stony branches of an Acropora. It may reach one meter in length and weigh 250 Kg.

D – A barracuda hovers in the shade of moored boats.

E – The giant trevally (Caranx ignobilis), a predator of the sea, swims near the surface in search of prey, often pushing toward shallow lagoons.

F – Hard corals grow in a way that allows each colony of polyps to receive enough sunlight to support the life of the symbiotic algae that give them their color and consistency.

Egyptian coast are the clearest evidence!

The surface portion of the reef is embellished with extensive umbrella Acropora structures that offer shelter to squirrelfish (*Sargocentron spiniferum*). These solitary inhabitants of the coral reef are red with yellowish fins. During the day you can find them sheltering in the protuberances of the wall. They come out at night to hunt their prey, small crustaceans and worms. Compact schools of striped anthias (*Pseudanthias taeniatus*) swim near the colonies of fire corals. The body of this serranid endemic to the Red Sea reaches 12 cm in length and has an

A

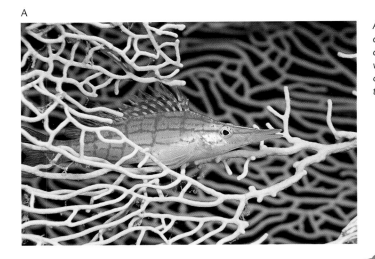

A – With its spiderweb color, the hawkfish can camouflage itself very well among the delicate branches of the gorgonians.

B – This young yellowedged lyretail (Variola louti), *sporting its youthful colors, is resting on a sponge. Note the delicate streaks of violet along the snout and gills.*

C – Another member of the Serranidae *family is the spotted grouper (Plectropomus pessuliferus). During the day, it usually lies in wait in the darker parts of the reef. Occasionally it can be admired in all its beauty as it swims through the open water.*

C

B

D

analyze the behavior of this small predator, who defends its hunting territory from competitors by attacking them and following them until they have left his territory. There are various cleaning stations in the southern part of Poseidon Reef, where fish of all species and sizes allow themselves to be groomed by cleaner wrasses, who remove parasites and patches of dead skin from their bodies. During my last exploration around the satellite tower of the main reef, I found an enormous giant trevally (*Caranx ignobilis*) over a meter long. This large pelagic fish was immobile, its branchial clefts open, with a whole team of cleaner wrasses swimming in and out of them. This unexpected and truly thrilling spectacle is one of the many sights that Poseidon Reef regularly offers.

D – A beautiful tête-à-tête with two hawkfish (Paracirrhites forsteri). *This sedentary species loves to lie in wait resting on the branches of* Pocillopora *or* Acropora *corals. The bicolor scales tell us that these are two young individuals.*

E – Flowering red alcyonarians embellish *the already extraordinary structure of this gorgonian. In areas more exposed to the current, which carries in more nourishment, coral life reaches its maximum splendor.*

unmistakable red color with a white stripe on the flanks and ventral area. It feeds on zooplankton and swims in darts, never leaving its territory, where various harems comprised of a male and numerous females coexist. One odd fact is that when the male of a family dies, the dominant female changes sex and replaces him. Various types of butterflyfish move in pairs in their incessant search for food, which leads them to continuously "peck" at the corals and tear off the polyps on which they feed. Around the main reef, the sandy bottom is about ten meters deep, and if you look carefully at the base of the coral mushrooms scattered all around, you can see numerous bluespotted ribbontail rays resting on the sand, and perhaps even a crocodile fish. Near the crevices in the wall, red coral groupers protect their feeding territory by aggressively hurling themselves at and threatening any "competitor" fish that may approach. It's extremely interesting to watch and

E

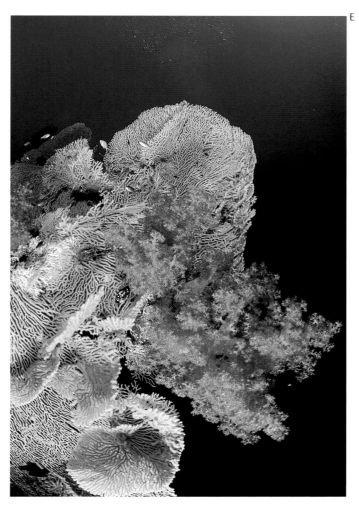

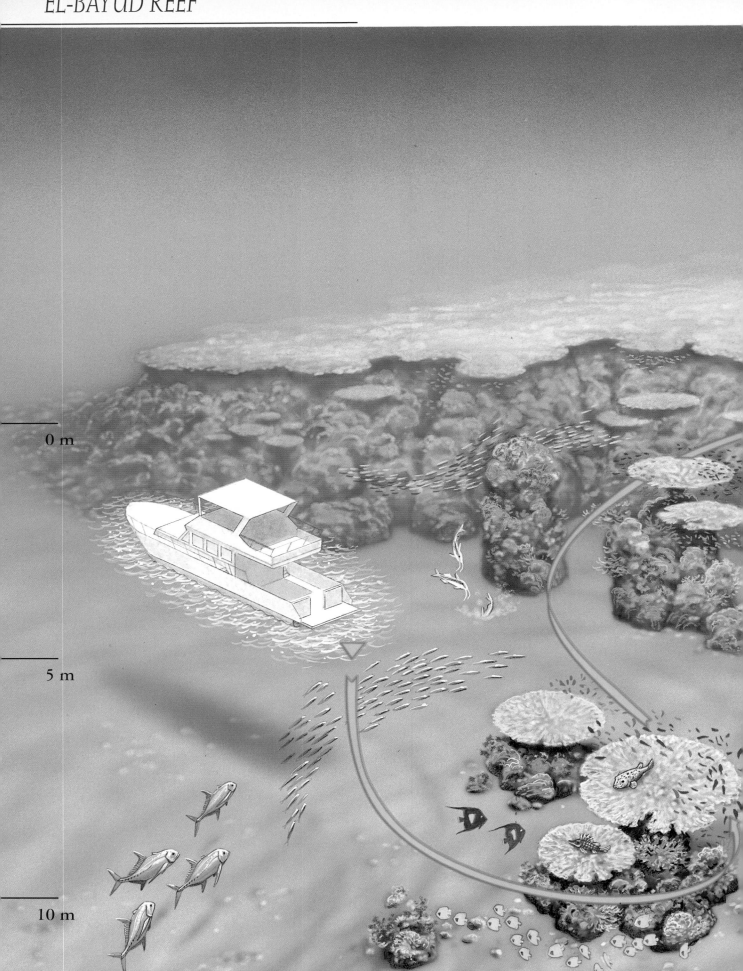

0 m

5 m

10 m

SHERATON

El-Bayud Reef

Off the coast where the El-Gouna hotel complex stands, a long chain of reefs run almost parallel with the land. This interesting coral formation, ideal for a snorkeling trip, is only a little over a half hour's sail from the dock of the TGI Diving Center. Due to the

A – To avoid damaging the sea bed with anchors, boats dock at fixed mooring lines.

B – A portion of the coral reef completely covered with formations of stony corals.

C – Turbinaria is highly complex in order to provide as much surface area as possible for the algae that keep it alive.

D – A hawkfish stands guard on the branches of a fire coral, which has extremely stinging tentacles.

E – The yellowband angelfish (Pomacanthus maculosus) is sociable and curious, but always stays a safe distance away.

F The Acropora corals this snorkeler is admiring have extraordinary, diverse forms. Branching corals are especially abundant in the upper part of the reef, offering shelter to a myriad of marine organisms.

A

B

C

relative vicinity of land, it's popular for short but pleasurable trips.

The sea is always calm and the boat uses a small anchor, always cast onto the sandy bottom to avoid damaging the reef, to moor near the coral barrier. The most interesting side of this underwater cordillera is to the northeast. It looks like a long coral road rising almost to the surface, with a sandy bottom about 4-6 meters deep. Blocks or small isolated pinnacles can be found along the entire perimeter of the reef. The coral garden is especially luxuriant, and the hard corals become truly enormous here. Deerhorn Acropora coral formations as tall as a man rise from the bottom, with pairs of butterflyfish swimming among their contorted arms. Some examples of Acropora florida resemble stone cactuses standing upright in the desert sand, in a truly lovely setting. Enormous blocks of velvety Porites have bulb anemones in their upper portions, and among their stinging tentacles move the highly territorial, odd-looking clownfish, who won't hesitate to approach you threateningly if you invade their privacy. You'll see numerous spotted angelfish, certainly one of the most beautiful fish in the Red Sea, their unmistakable blue color broken by a bright yellow vertical spot on their flanks. The hard corals are well-represented by splendid umbrella formations,

D

E

with the speed and precision of a raptor. You'll see dense schools of green damselfish that move in unison as if they were following mysterious commands. Approach them and they'll vanish to peep out among the tangled branches of the reef, gradually regrouping when they feel safe again.

In the open water, hundreds of fusiliers follow invisible particles of plankton in a constant search for food. They're always on the lookout for large jacks: these splendid predators hunt in groups, trying to isolate their prey from the school and push it toward the reef, making it more difficult to maneuver, and then mount an attack from all directions to catch it. Swimming on the surface with a mask, fins and mouthpiece, without interfering with the life of the reef in any way, you can see spectacular moments of animal life, and with a bit of sensitivity and knowledge, understand how the various species of fish interact with each other.

Don't forget to watch the sandy bottom as well, which like every tropical sea floor is full of life. You'll see large goatfish carefully inspecting the floor with their long whiskers; sometimes they slip halfway under the sand to follow the little invertebrates on which they feed. A trained and attentive eye may spot an expertly camouflaged crocodile fish, sometimes identifiable only by its large, ever-vigilant ocular bulbs.

F

forming tables up to two meters in diameter. It's not uncommon to see a pufferfish resting on its dense branches, mimicking its color in an attempt to pass unobserved. Be very careful when you swim near these marvelous but unfortunately very fragile coral formations. All it takes is a light blow to break the delicate, stem-like support that holds up the coral umbrella, destroying a masterpiece of Nature.

Groups of surgeonfish move in formation on the detrital bottom, sifting it in search of food and leaving a cloud of sand behind them.

Little hawkfish (*Paracirrhites forsteri*) always lie in ambush among the coral branches. Floating immobile as they await some small prey, they attack

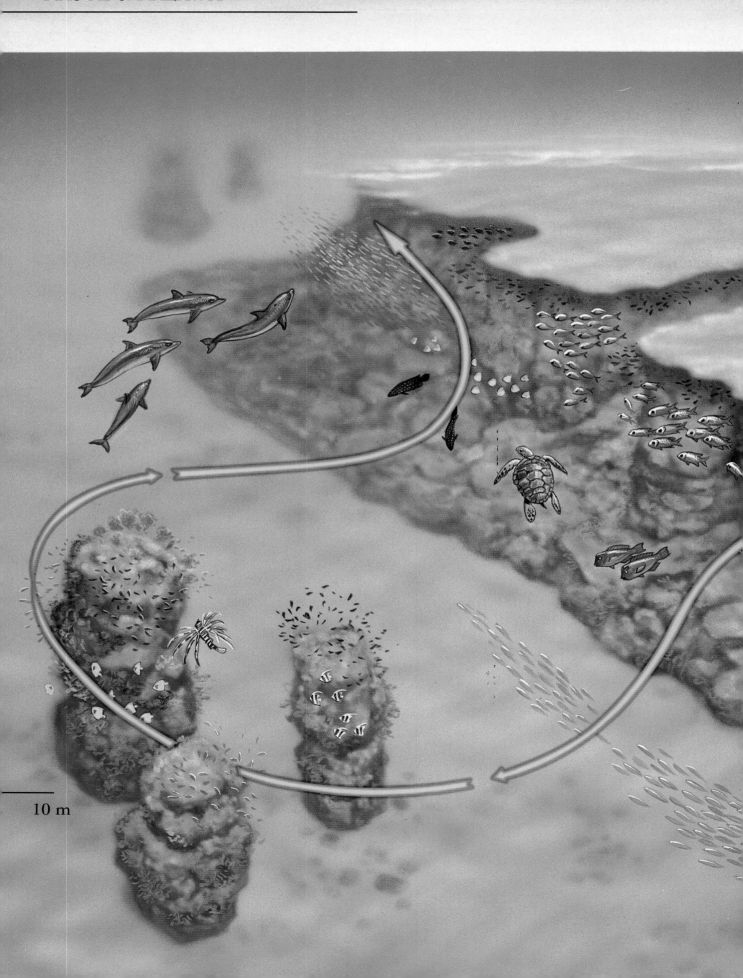

10 m

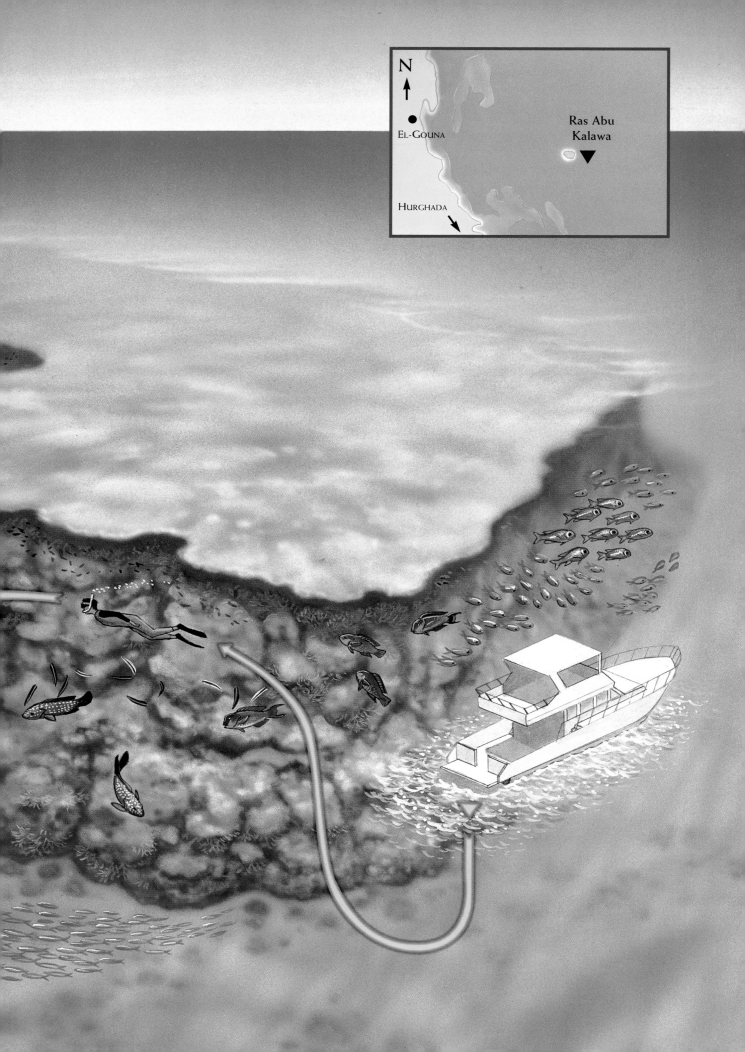

N

EL-GOUNA

HURGHADA

Ras Abu
Kalawa

Leaving the El-Gouna marina, sail southeast, and in a little less than an hour you'll reach your destination. Ras Abu Kalawa is not only an extraordinary place for snorkeling, but also an extremely interesting area for scuba diving.

When you arrive, tie the boat to one of the shamandura on the south side of the reef, which runs lengthwise from north to south, with an east wall running in an almost uninterrupted line to the north edge of the reef, where there are a couple of isolated coral blocks about ten meters from the central base. The west side has a group of deep recesses similar to small bays, and

F

D

E

A – A Pterois *has its dorsal spines erect in a defensive position. In case of danger, it can dart out with amazing speed.*

B – *The Abu Kalawa reef doubtless has one of the greatest varieties of species in the area. The coral formations protruding from the reef are colonized by stony corals.*

the southwest side has three extremely interesting hard coral towers that deserve a visit. The depth around the reef, which rises almost to the surface, is 12-14 meters on the east side and 6-8 meters on the opposite side. If there are currents, they'll be primarily northeast, but they create no special difficulties. You can snorkel around the coral reef in 40-50 minutes.

The two sides of Abu Kalawa are quite distinct from each other. The eastern side, with a light current that carries in nutrients for the coral polyps, is full of gorgonians growing perpendicular to the wall, thereby offering a greater surface for the flowing water that brings in plankton and thus life. Sheltered among the fans of the gorgonians, you can see well-camouflaged hawkfish (*Oxycirrhites typus*), *Pterois volitans* lazily resting on delicate, intricate lacework and small, rotating anthias (*Pseudanthias squamipinnis*). Coming closer to these splendid colonies, you'll see needlefish (*Corythoichthys sp.*) and tiny crabs scuttling through the formations. The wall is also embellished with tufts of brightly colored alcyonarians in shades running from red to pale yellow.

You'll feel like you're flying over a flowering garden, where the life forms seem to compete with each other in exhibiting the most bizarre

C – *A female parrotfish (Scarus gibbus) moves frenetically in search of corals to munch.*

D – *There are alcyonarians and red encrusting sponges on this splendid gorgonian fan. It's not unusual for the horny branches of gorgonians to be colonized by other coral forms like Alcyonaria.*

E – *Myriad life forms are concentrated along the walls more exposed to the flow of currents; the colorful branches of Alcyonaria, overlapping each other as they decorate the slope, look like explosions of color. The whole array of Red Sea fish parades incessantly before this backdrop.*

F – *The intricate branches of this red sponge offer shelter to numerous species of fish, including anthias. Formations of this type stand out from the vertical walls like cascades of color similar to the fronds of a plant. Spectacular yellow and black nudibranchs can often be seen on the branches.*

103

A

forms and colors. The whole range of reef fish seems to be represented here. Multicolored parrotfish (*Scarus sp.*) incessantly munch away at the corals, and after grinding up these "rocky" morsels and ingesting the algae they love, they release a fine stream of sand into the water that is deposited on the bottom. Pairs of masked butterflyfish (*Chaetodon semilarvatus*) show off their bright lemon yellow color, broken only by the dark mask around the eyes that gives them their name. Small wrasses swim endlessly among the crevices of the reef. The western side of the reef boasts a proliferation of rare hard corals, which have covered every inch of the surface area and the walls. Near the surface are groups of big-eye emperor angelfish (*Monotaxis grandoculis*) that watch your every movement, always keeping a safe distance away. Small red coral groupers appear to survey their territory and then return to the shadow of their dens. There are numerous "cleaning stations" near the reef's recesses, where fish of every type and size stop to be groomed by

cleaner wrasses (*Labroides dimidiatus*), which remove parasites and traces of food from between their teeth. It's a truly fascinating sight to watch these small fish literally swim into the mouths of their customers and come out of their branchial clefts like experienced dentists.

It's rather common to see sea turtles (*Eretmochelys imbricata*) tearing sponges from the floor with their strong beaks and swallowing them. When they're busy eating, these prehistoric-looking but completely harmless reptiles are easy to approach. But remember to never touch the animal for any reason!

The calm, shallow waters around Abu Kalawa are often frequented by a family of dolphins. If approached cautiously, without undue haste, you'll find it quite easy to observe them, and a younger one may curiously come very close. Ras Abu Kalawa is a magical place, with a reef so exciting that you won't want to leave the water.

B

C

C – A pair of bottlenose dolphins (Tursiops truncatus) plays on the sea bed. This species of mammal prefers shallow areas and lagoons, where it devotes itself to playing and looking after its young. Newborn dolphins are about one meter long and weigh about 15 kg.

A – Red alcyonarians have grown in the shelter of an Acropora, which is the most common stony coral colony in the Red Sea. It may vary greatly in form and size.

B – A cleaner wrasse (Labroides dimidiatus) removes parasites from the skin of a red coral grouper (Cephalopholis miniata).

D

E

D – A pair of butterflyfish (Chaetodon semilarvatus) takes shelter in a shadowy area below the coral formations. This species is found only in the Red Sea, and is one of the easiest coral fish to approach.

E – While sea turtles (Eretmochelys imbricata) are social animals, they are armed with long beaks.

F – Where the currents are strongest, gorgonians grow to spectacular sizes. Alcyonarians also colonize the fans exposed to the flow of plankton.

HURGHADA

Hurghada is about 600 kilometers south of Cairo. It has experienced an explosion in growth over recent years and is now considered the most important vacation area on the Egyptian coast. The city's construction began during the last century, in the same bay where the port of Myos Hormos was located in the Ptolemaic era. The underwater beauties of the reefs around the islands off the coast

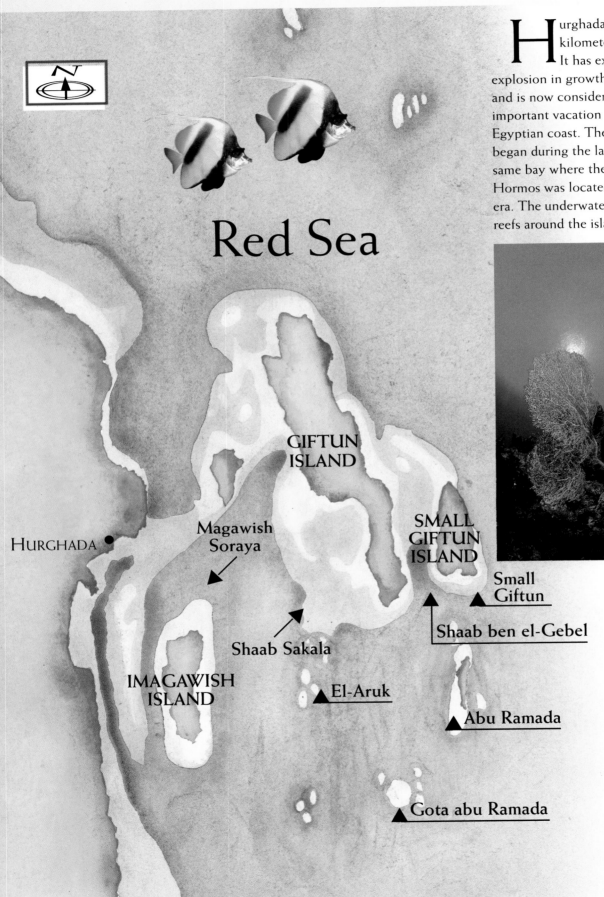

Red Sea

GIFTUN
ISLAND

Magawish
Soraya

HURGHADA ●

SMALL
GIFTUN
ISLAND

Small
Giftun

Shaab ben el-Gebel

Shaab Sakala

IMAGAWISH
ISLAND

▲ El-Aruk

▲ Abu Ramada

▲ Gota abu Ramada

A

A – The walls plunging down to the floor are embellished with an abundance of coral life: a gorgonian with a peculiar split form rises toward the sun, the source of life.

B – The islands off the coast of Hurghada offer spits of white sand that contrast with the turquoise water. The southern part of Giftun Island is a popular destination for a day of relaxation.

C – The seabeds of Hurghada offer magical sensations. A Pterois with fins similar to wings moves over a rare yellow gorgonian.

B

D – The beaches that run around the islands of the archipelago of Hurghada are frequented by sea turtles that lay their eggs here.
.
E – The island of Magawish Soraya can be reached in just a few minutes' sail. In the photograph, one of the boats has just unloaded its cargo of snorkelers into the water.

of Hurghada became known in the 1960s through a series of articles by the American biologist Eugenie Clark, later published by *National Geographic*; Clark had made a number of scientific expeditions to the area to document the wealth of the Red Sea's coral reef ecosystem. The construction of an international airport with connecting flights to major European cities significantly increased the number of seaside vacationers in the area. In the 1970s and 1980s, President Sadat strongly promoted tourism and economic development in the area. Since then, accommodation facilities have grown steadily, and now a string of vacation facilities stretches on for about twenty kilometers on the coast south of Hurghada. The enormous development over recent years has profoundly changed the face of the old port of Ghardaka, as it was known in ancient times. Today, Hurghada is a chaotic city with two fundamental

daily bring flocks of enthusiastic snorkelers to enjoy the beauty of this sea. The health of the reefs across from Hurghada is gradually improving due to HEPCA's protective policies; remember that until recently, over 300 boats transporting divers dropped anchor onto the reef every day, reducing to dust hundreds of square meters of precious coral. In 1992, several diving centers formed an organization known as HEPCA

D

E

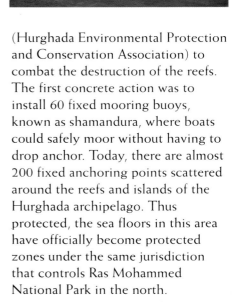

C

districts: the old port with the Sakkala quarter, and the modern business area of Dahar, located inland, which is popular with shoppers. Only rarely can you go snorkeling directly from the beaches across from the hotels, as the sandy bottom and shallow waters are not good for diving. Off the coast, however, there are semi-emerged reefs with spectacular coral walls and numerous islands where the reefs can be seen in all their splendor. Islands like Abu Ramada, Giftun, Magawish and Umm Gamar are now the destination of numerous boats that

(Hurghada Environmental Protection and Conservation Association) to combat the destruction of the reefs. The first concrete action was to install 60 fixed mooring buoys, known as shamandura, where boats could safely moor without having to drop anchor. Today, there are almost 200 fixed anchoring points scattered around the reefs and islands of the Hurghada archipelago. Thus protected, the sea floors in this area have officially become protected zones under the same jurisdiction that controls Ras Mohammed National Park in the north.

MAGAWISH SORAYA

0 m

3 m

6 m

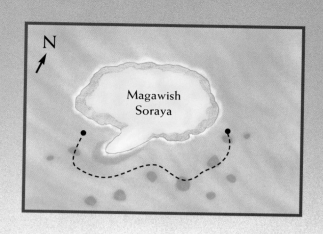

To the southwest of the island of Magawish, not particularly attractive to snorkelers, you'll find a little island whose floors can provide some pleasant, interesting excursions. Little Magawish can be reached from Hurghada in just over 30 minutes and is frequented daily by enthusiastic swimmers who explore its floors with masks and flippers for constantly fascinating encounters. The island, lying low on the water, is mostly rock with a few beaches. The tongue of sand on the south side that juts into the sea is gorgeous, with shades of color running from the blinding white sand to every shade of azure out to the deep blue sea. From one excursion across the surface to another, it's truly relaxing to bask in the warmth of the sun in one of the little bays in this tiny paradise. Moor the boat to one of the red anchoring buoys on the south side, over a sea floor 5 to 6 meters deep. The area can also be reached by glass bottom boats, giving those who can't dive the chance to enjoy the marvels of the underwater world. There are numerous coral blocks scattered on the bottom of this area. Located not far from each other, they rise toward the surface, little cathedrals surrounded by swarms of teeming life. In just a short time you can explore the whole circumference of the island, but the most interesting part is near the shamandura. As soon as you get into the water, you'll see sergeant majors (*Abudefduf saxatilis*) floating near the surface in dense groups, who will follow you fearlessly. Around the coral towers you'll see numerous species of stony corals in bizarre forms, surrounded by swarms of bluegreen tropical damselfish and the ever-present anthias, with vivid red-orange females and violet males. On the protuberances of the walls of the

pinnacles, soft corals grow in the form of small yellowish bushes that almost seem to sway with the wind. Sea anemones wave their tentacles on the sides exposed to the current, protected by clownfish (*Amphiprion bicinctus*) and driving off any fish who tries to approach their guest. This is an example of one of the most successful symbiotic relationships in the animal kingdom. Pairs of unmistakable yellow and black striped bannerfish (*Heniochus diphreutes*) survey the clusters of fire coral, which you should stay away from to avoid painful abrasions.

Colorful parrotfish move from one coral formation to another, continuously biting at the stony corals. If you get close enough, you can clearly hear the coral being crushed by their sturdy beaks. Resting on the sea floor, often partially covered by sand, you'll find bluespotted ribbontail rays (*Taeniura*

A – Even the first tip of the Red Sea breaker reef offers a truly unusual spectacle of life and colors.

B – The low islet of little Magawish rises from the crystalline waters. In the background, you can glimpse the long succession of hotels standing on the Hurghada coast.

C - Anthias (Pseudanthias squamipinnis) *populate the walls of the coral reefs to a depth of thirty meters. The group includes less colorful females and brighter males who may even be violet-hued.*

D – The tentacles of the sea anemone (Heteractis magnifica) *offer shelter to clownfish* (Amphiprion bicinctus), *with whom it lives in symbiosis.*

E - A huge Acropora *umbrella offers refuge to* a group of Red Sea bannerfish (Heniochus intermedius), *among whom swims an emperor angelfish* (Pomacanthus imperator).

lymma) waiting for dusk, when they'll head to shallow waters to hunt small crustaceans and mollusks, which they dig from the sand with rapid movements of their mantle. Other inhabitants of the sandy bottom that you can admire around the coral pinnacles include crocodile fish. Skillfully camouflaged but still visible if you look closely, they wait immobile for a small fish to carelessly venture too close, then fall upon it with unexpected agility and eat it in a

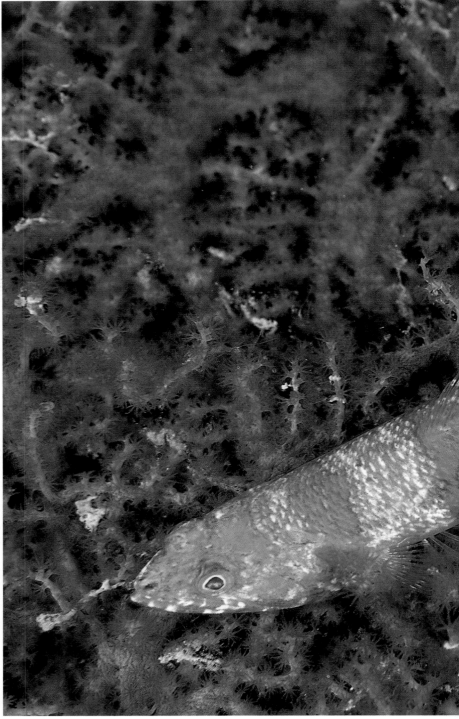

single gulp. Small groups of goatfish busily move the sand with their mobile barbels in search of food. It's easy to approach them as they wander along the detrital floor. Often you'll see dense schools of blue fusiliers passing by, easily recognizable by the black tips of their caudal fins, flowing like a river below and beside you as they follow invisible masses of plankton.

Despite the relative vicinity of a myriad of vacation facilities on the coast of Hurghada, this area is still fairly intact, and it's always pleasant to float over its coral outcroppings, watching the frenetic movement of the tropical reef from above.

In areas as calm and shallow as this, it's easy to concentrate on watching a single territorial species and try to understand its movements within the coral reef's fragile ecosystem.

A – Branched stony corals are a habitat for green chromis (Chromis viridis), who drive other fish from their territory.

B – Alcyonarians position themselves so they can receive clean water full of nutrients.

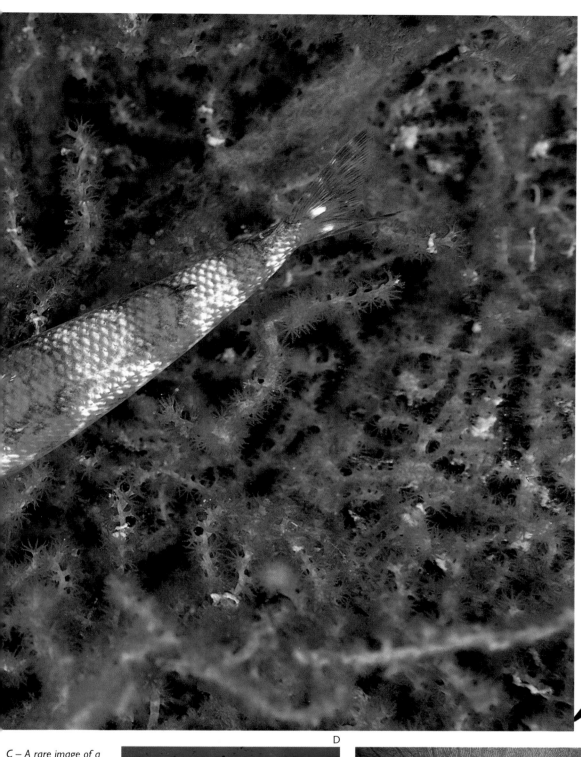

D – With their discoid, flattened bodies, rays have adapted to life on the sea floor; in this photograph, a bluespotted stingray (Taeniura lymma) digs in the sand with rapid movements of its mantle, uncovering the crustaceans and mollusks on which it feeds.

E – A group of yellow goatfish (Parupeneus cyclostomus) moves along the reef in search of small fish, which they flush from their dens with the long barbels on the sides of their mouths.

D

E

C – A rare image of a lizardfish (Synodus variegatus) lying in wait among the expanded polyps of a gorgonian. These fish usually live on the sea floor, using their skills of mimicry, and 'walk' on their sturdy ventral fins, which they use as feet.

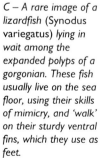

SHAAB SAKALA

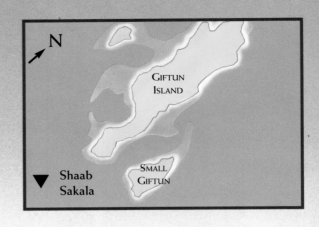

0 m

6 m

REEF

A – These alcyonarians (Dendronephthya), *with their pale pastel hues, have found a good place to filter water, settling on the stony supports of a gorgonian.*

B – A snorkeler is *swimming on the surface and admiring the wealth of marine life through crystal clear water.*

C – This blenny *(Ecsenius mida) helps make the underwater world an unforgettable place. It often intermingles with anthias to catch the plankton it finds suspended in the water.*

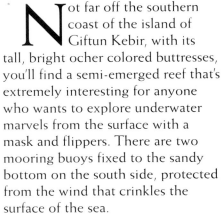

N ot far off the southern coast of the island of Giftun Kebir, with its tall, bright ocher colored buttresses, you'll find a semi-emerged reef that's extremely interesting for anyone who wants to explore underwater marvels from the surface with a mask and flippers. There are two mooring buoys fixed to the sandy bottom on the south side, protected from the wind that crinkles the surface of the sea.

The underwater foundation is rather irregular, with numerous crevices that form little inlets. Near the mooring lines, a block of isolated coral can serve as your starting point. The whole surface of the reef, where there is more sunlight, is embellished with a multitude of stony coral formations. Stony corals are well represented by the *Porites*. The hemispherical surface and soft contours of these colonies, which can reach several meters in diameter, is often interrupted by a small giant clam, its

B

mantle so vividly colored that it looks like a precious stone set into an equally precious jewel. The calcareous mass is etched by deep furrows caused by bites from parrotfish, who munch on the outer portion of the stony coral to remove the layer of algae that covers it, a fundamental part of their diet. In fact, you'll see a continuous bustle of parrotfish, especially *Scarus gibbus*, whose color varies depending on its sex. Females are yellowish with green areas near the tail and below the mouth, while males have green scales with some purple areas, especially on the head. There are also soft broccoli corals (*Lythophiton arboreum*), which indeed look like broccoli and are olive green in color. These alcyonarians are quite robust and can even live on muddy floors where the water is murky. They can reach the respectable size of 60 centimeters. It's not uncommon to see a few sea turtles (*Eretmochelys imbricata*), which are often spotted as they busily pull off sponges or alcyonarians from the sea floor. With a little patience, you can wait until the turtle leaves the floor to take a breath of air at the surface. If you move very slowly and carefully, you can come quite close to these splendid creatures, which unfortunately have become increasingly rare in these seas. Half hidden on the sandy floor, you can

C

D – Corals that grow *close to the surface may emerge during low tide, but protect themselves from the sunlight by secreting special substances that filter ultraviolet rays.*

E – Butterflyfish *(Chaetodon semilarvatus) are sedentary and gregarious. Some form pairs that stay together for many years, unless outside forces separate them.*

F – Clownfish *(Amphiprion bicinctus) live in pairs, with the female the larger of the species.*

A

D

E

F

see beautiful examples of crocodile fish (*Papilloculiceps longiceps*) and bluespotted ribbontail rays (*Taeniura lymma*), typical inhabitants of detrital areas.

If you look closely, you'll certainly find a tasseled scorpionfish (*Scorpaenopsis oxycephala*) immobile on a protrusion of the wall, relying on its perfect mimicry to attract prey, which it captures with a rapid leap forward, mouth open. Squirrelfish (*Sargocentron spiniferum*) peep out curiously from the cavities in the wall. Showing off their brilliant red color, solitary emperor angelfish (*Pomacanthus imperator*) swim near the surface, and all around is a riot of small, brightly colored inhabitants of the coral reef, from wrasses to butterflyfish, red groupers to surgeonfish. This area is visited infrequently, and thus the corals are in excellent condition. Try to leave everything intact in this fragile ecosystem that makes the Red Sea coral reefs a heritage for us all.

EL-ARUK

0 m

5 m

10 m

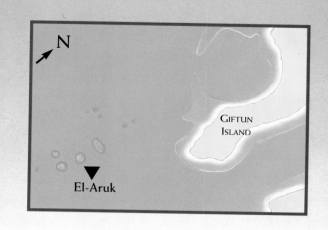

A

Your destination is a little over one hour's sail from Hurghada. South of the beautiful beach of Big Giftun and west of the island of Abu Ramada with its sandy bottom about 10-12 meters deep, you'll see a group of coral towers rising from the floor, forming a sort of colonnade that varies in size and arrangement. The Arabic word *aruk* is simply the plural of *erg*, which means a coral formation similar to a tower, rising almost to the surface. This area is scattered with small, circular, stony coral formations in a myriad of sizes and shapes that in some cases rise up from the floor almost to the water's surface. There are three main areas of *ergs*: Aruk Diana to the southwest, comprised of 7 towers, Aruk Mansur to the northeast, formed of about ten ergs, and a central portion including 6-7 buttresses called El-Aruk Giftun. With mask and flippers, this is where you'll begin your exploration of the sea bed! Moving around the surface areas of these formations is like swimming in a fantastic aquarium where the shallow depth and extraordinary brightness of the environment make your trip truly exciting. You can anchor the boat to one of the mooring buoys on the south side of the *ergs*. The towers are not far apart, and after your swim around the first one, lift your head out of the water to find the next one, swim toward it, and proceed to explore the entire area. The concentration of coral life is spectacular, and clouds of red anthias

welcome you, swimming near stony coral formations that rival each other for odd forms and colors. The central tower may be one of the most beautiful, and is broken by a deep crevice where you can see swarms of glassfish sheltered, moving compactly like an army of tiny transparent soldiers. The walls are richly decorated by delicate alcyonarians in pale pastel hues and other soft yellow corals. There are also many gorgonians growing perpendicular to the vertical wall so that they can offer the greatest possible surface area to the nutrient-rich current. Skillfully camouflaged among them are numerous *Pterois volitans*, which you can sometimes see swimming near the surface with slow movements that make them look more like birds than fish. You'll frequently see large angelfish such as *Pomacanthus maculosus*, its electric blue color broken by a yellow spot that makes it stand out from the multitude of fish that converge in this area. The great number of fish moving around the towers attracts numerous predators like trevallies, who

B

C

A, B – The more shadowy portions of the reef are colonized by shade-loving organisms like soft corals. As they have no calcareous structure, their structure is gelatinous.

C – A starfish (Fromia monilis) is attacking an encrusting red sponge, whose flesh makes a tasty dinner.

D – A crown-of-thorns (Acanthaster planci) is positioning itself on a raspberry coral (Pocillopora verrucosa). Acanthasters use powerful gastric juices to feed on coral polyps. It poses a serious threat to the coral reef.

E – Many Red Sea coral reefs are known as "breaker reefs." Waves limit coral growth on the upper portion, but the underwater portion is a riot of color.

D

swim swiftly from one *erg* to another, and large groupers that can be seen lying in ambush in the more shadowy areas of the reef. The bright colors of the butterflyfish will accompany you throughout your dive, and if you watch the sandy areas among the formations you may see large triggerfish (*Balistoides viridescens*) who, head down, blow water onto the floor to uncover crustaceans and mollusks for a tasty snack. Your exploration from the surface is quite varied and relaxing, and you'll have some spectacular sights. You should really avoid going to El-Aruk on windy days when the sea is rough, as underwater visibility is greatly reduced. The area is often swept by powerful currents, so check your position to be sure not to drift too far.

SMALL GIFTUN

0 m

6 m

GIFTUN ISLAND

SMALL GIFTUN

N

REEF SECTION

A – Dense schools of surgeonfish (Naso unicornis), with adults who can be distinguished by the horn between their eyes.

B – An angelfish (Pomacanthus maculosus) is feeding on the polyps of an alcyonarian.

C – Various species of butterflyfish intermingle. A pair of Heniochus intermedius and one of Caethodon semilarvatus can be recognized in the image.

D – A lovely gorgonian, with what looks like fallen snow above it, has settled on a massive colony of mosaic coral (Favia favus).

Off the coast of Hurghada are the islands of Giftun Kebir (Big Giftun), and, to the southeast, Giftun el-Saghir (Little Giftun). The itinerary winds through the southern part of Little Giftun. You'll reach your destination after about a one hour sail east.

Moor the boat in the shelter of the reef on the south side of the island's eastern tip. Here you will find numerous fixed mooring lines, and sea conditions are usually perfect for a snorkeling expedition. Visibility is good unless there is a strong wind, when the sea is rough and sand clouds the water. The sandy floor is 5-7 meters below the keel of the boat, and before you you'll see several coral buttresses that rise almost to the surface. The coral formations continue to the island's main reef, which is detached from the beach, forming a swimming pool connected to the open sea. The sand on the bottom reflects the sunlight, glinting from the surface.

Your "stroll" will take you on an exploration of the walls of the coral towers near the surface. The first thing

A

you'll note is the concentration of anthias swimming near the reef, ready to seek refuge in the crevices at the first sign of danger. Their red-orange color makes them one of the nicest species to watch. In the shelter of the little terraces formed by coral protrusions, you can see sweetlips (Plectorhinchus gaterinus) waiting for night to fall so they can move to shallow waters to search the seabed for the little invertebrates on which they feed. You'll see parrotfish absorbed in biting the coral reef: it's interesting to watch them use their horny beaks to attack the coral and feed on the polyps and algae that comprise it. Butterflyfish are well represented, and you'll see many pairs

E – From the boat moored near the coral reef south of the island of Giftun, the stony coral "cordillera" can be clearly seen that surrounds the lagoon with its turquoise waters.

F – A hawkfish is perched on the top of a stony coral, waiting for careless preys.

G – The life of the coral reef conceals complex relationships between one organism and another, making it difficult to understand the balances that govern this delicate ecosystem.

E

F

G

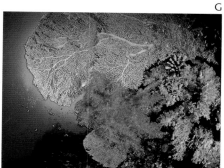

circling about in search of food. Sea anemones (*Heteractis magnifica*) have grown on the ridges, with tentacles that provide shelter for families of clownfish (*Amphiprion bicinctus*). When the anemones are disturbed, they retract their tentacles and disappear into the fissures of the wall to which

they are attached. The sandy floor contains crocodilefish and spotted rays. The bright light and good position of these circular reefs offer you a chance to admire a rich coral environment. Small, delicate alcyonarians in pale pastel hues reach out to the open sea to capture

plankton; delicate gorgonian fans grow in the areas where the current is stronger. Small, timid, green and black chromis move among the branches of *Acropora* corals. Don't neglect the outer part of the reef that delimits the lagoon; you may be lucky enough to see a sea turtle.

SHAAB BEN EL-GEBEL

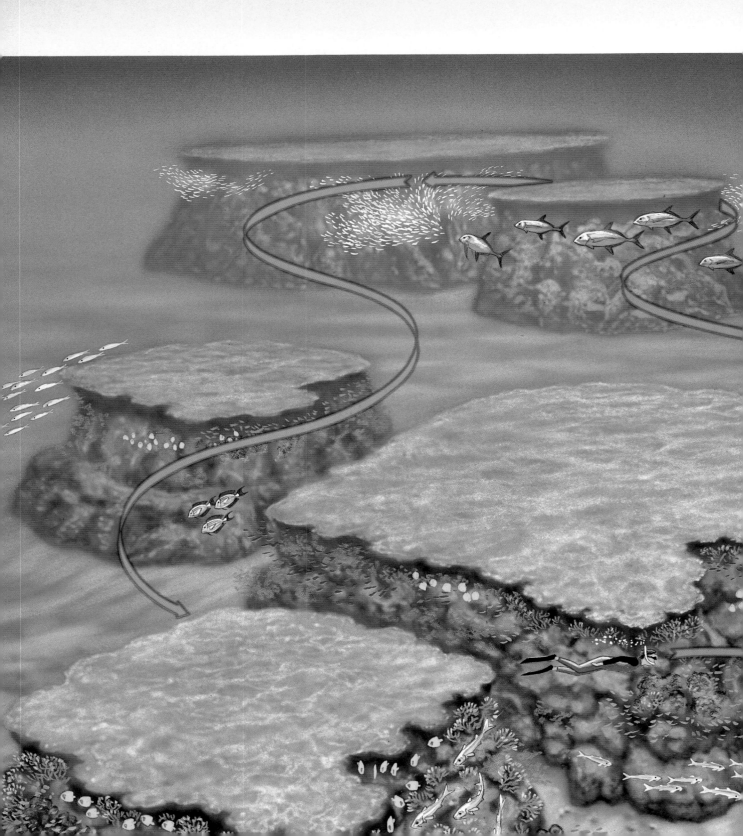

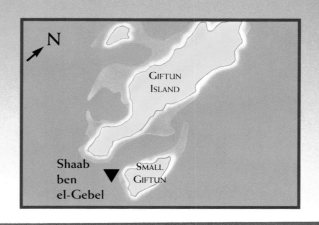

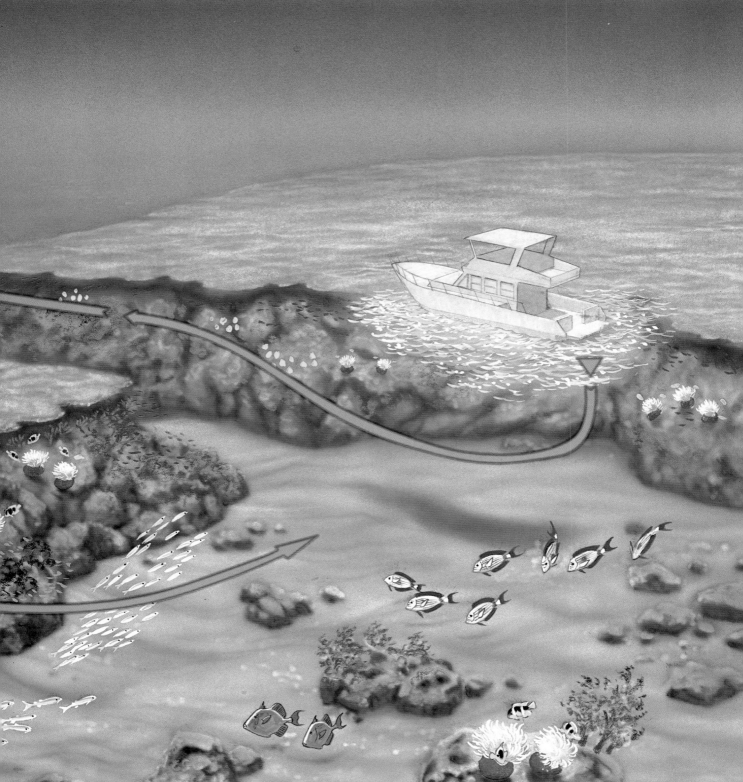

T his popular site for snorkelers is a little over one hour's sail from the coast of Hurghada. In Arabic, the name of the area means "reef between the mountains," and in fact the coral district you'll be visiting is in the strait between the tall buttresses of the islands of Giftun Soraya and Giftun

A – The luminous water and rich plankton life guarantee optimal conditions for the growth of corals.

B – Soft corals have a flexible trunk that supports clusters of polyps that open at night.

C – Reef-building polyps can build colonies that develop in compact calcareous masses or fragile formations that can become several meters long. The image shows an Acropora sea fan.

D – The coral platform of Shaab ben el-Gebel is between the two islands of Giftun.

E – Butterflyfish have a flattened body with a band of color near the eye. This is a Chaetodon melannotus.

F – A hawkfish peers out from the formations of a Tubastrea. This stony coral forms arborescent colonies and needs sunny waters to grow.

Kebir. Not far off is the beautiful Giftun beach, where you can relax between dives. Moor your boat on the south side of the reef, sheltered from the wind and the waves, over a sandy floor about 6-7 meters deep. The stony coral formation you'll be exploring is an extensive, elongated table similar to a stubby banana, with a floor that varies from 4 to 10 meters

deep rising almost to the water's surface. The side facing west is marked by deep inlets that form tranquil lagoons with a myriad of coral fish. Not far from the slope facing south, you'll see several similar-looking ergs shaped like low pyramids with cut-off tops, rising from the floor to 2-3 meters from the surface. You can begin your trip by surveying these

towers, which are surrounded by a large variety of creatures. In particular, the shallower portion of the clusters is inhabited by swarms of glassfish, in constant movement to confuse natural predators such as bluefin trevallies (Caranx melampygus): it's quite interesting to note how the rapid, coordinated movements of the little glassfish disorient predators,

D

E

their wake like a stream of smoke, followed closely by various types of small *Labridae* in search of some edible leftovers. The portion of the reef most illuminated by the sun is colonized by flourishing colonies of *Pocillopora* stony corals, whose purple branches host families of green chromis (*Chromis viridis*). Pairs of masked butterflyfish (*Chaetodon semilarvatus*) float immobile below any shelter the wall can offer, and are certainly among the most colorful endemic species of the Red Sea. When you've circumnavigated half the coral massif, turn back to your starting point, following the contour of the reef, which will lead

F

who are unable to focus on just one individual. In most cases the attack fails. The walls are also embellished by an assortment of soft corals, with colors that are not extremely bright but forms that are quite varied. Your exploration will take you to the main body of the reef, and keeping it to your left, you'll head north. There are a number of sea anemones on the vertical walls, inhabited by numerous harems of clownfish. If you come too close, they'll take refuge within the stinging tentacles of their host. Groups of striped surgeonfish (*Ctenochaetus striatus*) move along the sandy floor, dragging their long flexible teeth across it to uncover the detritus they like to eat. They leave suspended particles in you to deep, narrow inlets where you'll find large schools of yellowfin goatfish (*Mulloides vanicolensis*). Along the entire route, you'll see that the upper area of the reef is literally covered with dense colonies of fire coral (*Millepora dichotoma*). Be very careful not to brush against the tips of these hydrozoans, or you'll get a painful burn.

0 m

5 m

10 m

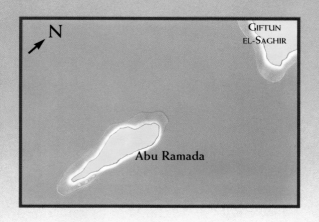

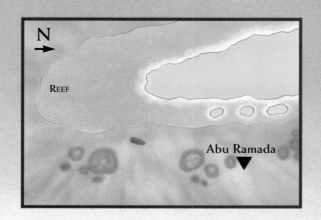

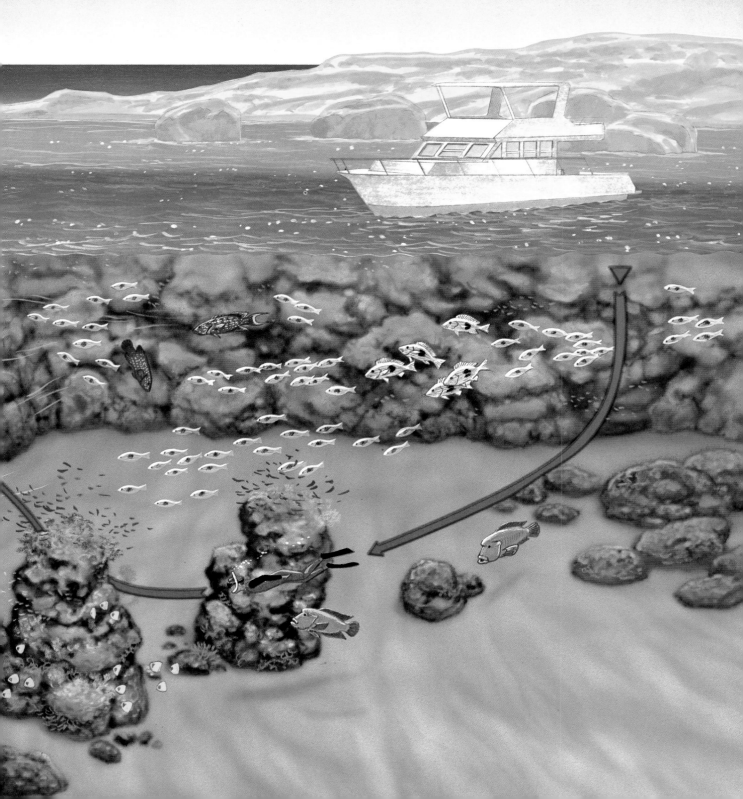

A little over one hour's sail away from the coast, you'll come to Abu Ramada, the southernmost, outermost island of the Hurghada archipelago. It's a long, narrow, rocky formation located south of the two islands of Giftun. The south side provides optimal conditions for a tranquil excursion of the surface. The southern side of Abu Ramada is well sheltered from the winds that blow constantly from the north, and boats can find shamandura, or mooring lines, for a stable anchorage here. Three masses of land and a long tongue of rock extend from the main body of the island. The surface reef then extends for many meters until reaching a vertical drop-off that falls to a sandy plateau about 5-6 meters deep. Several stony coral formations rise from the detrital floor, forming true oases of life in the sand. You can begin your exploration by observing the summits of the towers, which in most cases are cleaning stations where cleaner wrasses (*Labroides dimidiatus*) groom fish much larger than themselves by removing parasites from them. Cleaner wrasses are about ten centimeters long, have a tapered body that is blue with a black band down their flanks, and a small pointed mouth. They swim in jerks in a sort of dance that makes them recognizable to their "customers,"

A – Where the currents are more powerful, gorgonians are denser, larger and more robust, reaching up to three meters in width.

B – The nutrient-rich waters that lap the reef of Abu Ramada encourage the luxuriant growth of soft corals.

C – A yellowbelly damselfish (Amblyglyphidodon leucogaster) patrols its territory, moving among the petrified structures of a dead gorgonian.

D – Clownfish (Amphiprion bicinctus) can live among stinging tentacles by covering their bodies with mucus. The anemone recognizes the mucus of its guest and refrains from striking with its stinging cells.

A

who remain motionless, mouth open, to allow the little fish to enter and remove parasites from their gills. It's extremely interesting to see how large fish like trevallies, groupers or surgeonfish change color while being cleaned, as if to show their satisfaction for the service received! The open water between the pinnacles and the wall is frequented by numerous cornetfish (*Fistularia commersonii*), with a very elongated body and a long cornet-shaped mouth that they use to suck up their prey. Their color can vary depending on the surrounding environment, making them a champion of mimicry in the Red Sea. You'll often encounter

humphead wrasses (*Cheilinus undulatus*) as well, who will curiously approach snorkelers and watch them with their protruding, highly mobile ocular globes. At the base of the wall you'll find dense schools of blackspotted snappers (*Lutjanus ehrenbergi*) moving in disorderly fashion as if following invisible paths. These robust predators spend their days near the protrusions of the reef and can easily be recognized by the large black spot in the mid-section of their silvery bodies, traversed by narrow yellowish streaks. Keeping the edge of the reef to your right and swimming for a few meters, you'll see the wreck of a boat resting on a sandy floor about

E   F

6-7 meters deep. Sunk not long ago, it has now become a shelter for many creatures who have made it home. You can see numerous groupers patrolling their territory, and a large moray scrutinizes the area outside its cave. You'll also see purple anthias and the whole range of tropical fish typical of the zone. Small trevallies slip through the structures of the ship, which sank in an upright position, hoping to surprise some unwary fish and fall upon it in a lightning attack. A permanent resident of the ship's hold is a comical-looking porcupinefish (*Diodon bistrix*), which often seems to rest on the outside of the ship as if it were a member of the crew!

E – The waters that bathe the southern shores of the island of Abu Ramada are tranquil and an ideal place for snorkeling.

F – A Porites stony coral formation looks like a solidified lava flow. The polyps of this stony coral generally expand at night and are extremely small, with a very slow growth rate of about one centimeter a year.

GOTA ABU RAMADA

0 m

6 m

12 m

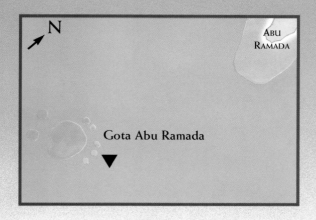

N

ABU
RAMADA

Gota Abu Ramada

▼

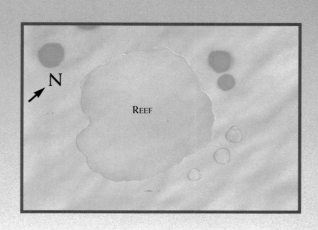

N

REEF

A little over a mile away from the southern tip of the island of Abu Ramada is one of the most spectacular reefs in the area, where the marine fauna you can see is so abundant and varied that it deserves its nickname of Aquarium. It's about an hour sail from Hurghada, and when you get there, all you have to do is choose one of the various buoys on the south side to moor your boat. Before you, you'll see a large, semi-emerged, elliptical reef about 200 meters in diameter at its widest part. There are two large coral towers about 10 meters high, standing like

A

B

satellites of the main coral base about 15 meters from the wall of the gota, and along the northeast section are four smaller pinnacles. The water around the gota varies in depth from 9 to 12 meters.

As it is mostly frequented by scuba divers with breathing apparatus who dive near the sea floor, the upper reef is perfectly intact and full of all species of stony corals. The bright light sets off the

A – This scorpionfish (Scorpaenopsis barbata) *has assumed a red color. Scorpiaenidae, masters of mimicry, normally assume the color of the sea bed on which they are resting.*

B – *This moray* (Gymnothorax javanicus), *a member of the order Anguilliformes, normally spends the daylight hours in its den. Morays may reach up to three meters in length.*

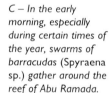

C

E

delicate structures built by the coral polyps, in an incessant work that has gone on for millennia. You'll see a large number of different *Acropora* species, from those that grow like tables parallel to the surface to those that rise upward in intricate branching formations. You'll also find compact, spherical brain coral traversed by furrows that look like the maze of a labyrinth, and small groups of beautiful dark red raspberry coral. The wall doesn't drop straight down, but is furrowed by deep cracks that resemble small canyons, whose walls are completely colonized by every form of benthic coral organisms. Begin exploring along the north wall, where at a depth of about 2 meters you'll find crevices similar to fractures running horizontally across the wall. Inside these cavities you'll see a number of whitefin sharks (*Triaenodon obesus*), who rest during the day in anticipation of their

C – *In the early morning, especially during certain times of the year, swarms of barracudas* (Spyraena sp.) *gather around the reef of Abu Ramada.*

D – *The movements of dense swarms of glassfish* (Parapriacanthus guentheri) *follow very precise patterns. A compact school is a form of defense for this species.*

E – *During the day, yellowfin goatfish* (Mulloides vanicolensis) *gather in groups that move carefully along the reef. If you approach them slowly, you can swim through the school without causing it to disperse.*

F – *This alcyonarian's decorative form embellishes its section of the coral reef. Soft corals feed on plankton carried in by the currents.*

D

F

nightly hunting forays. Despite their fierce appearance, they're harmless, and if left undisturbed can be observed without problem.

Continue your exploration westward, keeping the reef to your left. At about three meters deep, you'll find schools of goatfish (*Mulloides vanicolensis*), their bodies streaked with yellow and silvery

horizontal stripes. They live in such dense groups that they look like living walls. It's intoxicating to cross one of these compact formations during a dive, fragmenting it like the shards of an explosion, only to see it regroup behind you.

Passing swarms of sergeant majors who reflect silvery light, glide over the expanse of sand that separates the wall from the two imposing ergs on the west side. The towers are traversed by numerous cracks, within which you can see clouds of glassfish (*Parapriacanthus guentheri*). These little inhabitants of the reef cavities move in unison at the slightest provocation, and during the day remain hidden from

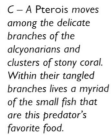

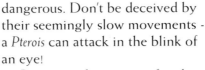

A – Large coral formations offer many forms of shelter for different species. Gota Abu Ramada is famous for its stony coral mushrooms teeming with life.

B – Trevallies (Caranx sexfasciatus) can quickly follow schools of small fish, surround them, and attack.

C – A Pterois moves among the delicate branches of the alcyonarians and clusters of stony coral. Within their tangled branches lives a myriad of the small fish that are this predator's favorite food.

D – The towers built by Porites stony corals have made Gota Abu Ramada famous. They hold hundreds of butterflyfish, which usually live in pairs and gather only when they are in sea portions abundant in food.

A

dangerous. Don't be deceived by their seemingly slow movements - a Pterois can attack in the blink of an eye!

Return to the main reef and explore the curves of the south side of the wall. Particular current movements bring large amounts of plankton to this area, naturally followed by bands of fusiliers, who swim with their mouths open to ingest as much as possible. In the open sea, bands of trevallies with their massive silver heads are always on the prowl.

Approaching the moored boats, you'll notice hundreds of striped surgeonfish (Ctenochaetus striatus) under their keels. It's an unusual and quite entertaining sight to watch them intently grazing the planks for encrusting algae. Continuing east, you may see large morays swimming in the open water, slithering with snakelike bodies through the protrusions on the sea floor. Finally, you'll come

B

C

possible predators. Along the walls grow soft alcyonarians, and a myriad of gorgonians embellish the scene with their fans. You'll see a number of Pterois volitans around the two ergs. Resting on the coral, they gather all their fins around their bodies in order to appear as inanimate as possible, thus deceiving some small prey. Or you may see them near the water's surface, showing off their feathery fins in all their splendor, making them one of the most spectacular and strangest residents of the coral reef. Remember not to come too close and never disturb these splendid creatures, as their poisonous stingers are extremely

to the northeast side with its pinnacles. The entire Abu Ramada gota contains a quantity and variety of fish difficult to find anywhere else, but this area of the reef is at its best. Hundreds of Red Sea bannerfish (Heniochus intermedius) surround large Porites coral

formations. Sometimes you'll find them layered and mixed with bands of masked butterflyfish (Chaetodon semilarvatus), species that are usually only seen in pairs. But there's more of everything at Gota Abu Ramada. The fish are more numerous, and even their colors seem brighter and more vivid than usual. Near the floor are incredible groups of grunts (Plectorhinchus gaterinus), with their splendid yellow scales dotted with black spots. They move lazily near small caves that are already occupied by groups of small yellowtail barracudas moving slowly like a compact silvery mass. On the sandy floor, small bluespotted ribbontail rays move from one shelter to another, leaving clouds of sand in their wake. Places like these offer a feast for your eyes in a constant variety of spectacular scenes. Be very careful how you move when you're near the reef. In particular, when you're in a vertical position, don't forget that you're wearing flippers, which could lead you to misjudge your distance from the corals. Remember that even though these microorganisms look rocky, they are extremely fragile. Be careful to ensure that natural sanctuaries like this remain intact so future generations can admire them too.

A wonderful undersea world

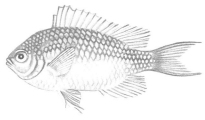

The Red Sea, from Suez to the Strait of Bab al Mandab, lies in a narrow depression whose unique environmental characteristics have helped make it one of the most important natural sites in the world. To the north, it's divided into two narrow arms separated by the Sinai Peninsula: the Gulf of Suez, with shallow, sandy seabeds, and the Gulf of Aqaba, which is up to 1400 meters deep. A number of interacting conditions such as the exceptional luminosity, the absence of rivers, scant rainfall, and temperatures that never drop below 20 degrees Centigrade (beyond which the coral polyps could not survive) have contributed to making the coral reef exceptionally large. The sharp contrast between the underwater and land environments is surprising; the more lifeless the deserts and mountains that overlook this sea, the more explosive and teeming with activity is the underwater life. The Red Sea reefs you'll be interested in exploring are the so-called coastal reefs, which are no more than 50 meters deep and lie not far offshore.

Continuously growing, albeit only a few centimeters a year, with countless cracks and fissures and interspersed with detrital and sandy areas, they make an ideal habitat for the marine organisms that populate this fantastic world. The coral reef is the product of the ceaseless work of *Coelenterata*, the polyps of stony corals, who constantly build calcareous skeletons on which they can form new colonies of their species, and where almost all inhabitants of the sea find food and refuge in their eternal struggle for survival. Of the over 170 species of coral that have been classified in the waters of the Red Sea, stony corals are what snorkelers most commonly see. The distribution of the various species depends on light, currents and waves. Near the coast, there are colonies with stubby branches from the *Pocilloporidae* family.

As you go farther out, you'll see a greater proliferation of colonies from the *Favidae* family, easily recognizable by the orderly, honeycomb-like form of the corallites. The outer areas, which are more exposed to the movement of the water, are colonized by the *Acropora* family, with 15

species in the Red Sea. They are considered the finest of stony corals. Where the water is shallower, they have well-developed branches known as "staghorns," while in deeper water they assume a typical table or umbrella form supported by a calcareous column. Next to hermatypic, or reef-building corals, there are the so-called soft corals. Although their participation in the construction process is not evident, they are very important to the coral environment. The better known types are the gorgonians and alcyonarians. Their structure consists of gelatinous cells strengthened by calcareous spicules that support the colony when it is large. These spicules are clearly visible in species from the genus *Dendronephthya*, which is quite common and forms marvelous splashes of color along the reef. The polyps are grouped together and seem to form colorful blooms. The large fans of the gorgonians, oscillating with the waves, actually grow perpendicular to the current in order to take maximum advantage of the nutritive substances they transport. Fire corals deserve special mention. With their highly stinging nematocysts, they are an insidious danger, so you should learn to recognize them so you can avoid accidentally touching them. This marvelous ecosystem, home to a multitude of animal species, has several enemies. The first is *Acanthaster planci*, or the crown-of-thorns starfish. This member of the *Asteroidea* family can digest the polyps, leaving only the calcareous skeleton. Other fish who graze on coral are parrotfish, who use their robust horny plates to tear off pieces so they can feed on the zooxanthellae, the algae that live in symbiosis with the polyps by photosynthesizing nutritive substances. Surgeonfish and a multitude of butterflyfish feed not only on encrusting algae, but also on the polyps, which they seize with their elongated mouth apparatus. Of the fish that live in this ecosystem, it's

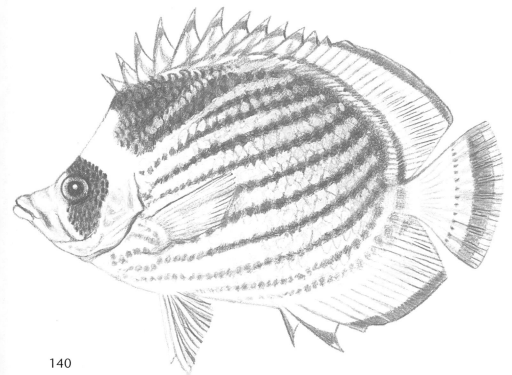

impossible to make a clear distinction between coral and pelagic fish, because many of the latter change their habits, depending on their stage of life or needs. A typical example is the *Carangidae* family, fish which are usually pelagic, but who often come to the reef in search of food, or the barracudas, who are gregarious and live near the reef when young, but become solitary as adults and swim in the open sea.

The fantastic architectures constructed by reef-building corals are doubtless the first thing you'll notice as you look down into the water, but the fish will soon capture your attention. There are about a thousand species of fish in the Red Sea. Of these, about fifteen percent are endemic, i.e. are found only here. With so many species, it's difficult to find a common thread for identifying

them. The most gaudy inhabitants of the reef are certainly the *Pomacanthidae*, or angelfish. No other family is as brightly colored, and it's common to see these living palettes of color swimming alone along the reef. Another amusing inhabitant of this sea is the humphead wrasse, which is a member of the *Labridae* family. It's a true giant that can often be seen in the company of the tiny cleaner wrasse, from the same family. There are numerous colorful parrotfish in the upper portions of the reef. Their color changes depending on their age and sex, and they are always intent on breaking off pieces of stony coral with their robust beaks. The great triggerfish, whose head accounts for about a third of its entire body, commonly frequents detrital areas, where it searches for food and builds its nests during the

reproduction period. Triggerfish have been found to exhibit learned behavior patterns based on past experience. One member of the large family of herbivores is the surgeonfish, which has sharp blades on the caudal peduncle that it uses for self-defense. The family of butterflyfish is extremely common. You'll be attracted to their bright colors as you see them swimming in pairs among the crevices of the reef.

The coral reef is a delicate ecosystem with an extremely fragile balance that small, seemingly irrelevant changes can affect with disastrous results. Any blow with your flipper or sharp movement that breaks a piece of coral can cause injuries that may take decades to repair. Even superficial knowledge of the world you'll be visiting will help you to fully enjoy its marvels: don't forget that knowledge generates respect.

Gray Reef Shark - *Carcharhinus amblyrhynchos*

Medium-sized shark with tapered body and elongated, rounded snout. The body is dark gray on the back, gradually lightening until it becomes whitish on the stomach. The dorsal fin is semi-falcate, and the rounded tip is white, as is the apex of the pectoral fins. Young individuals love surface waters. It feeds on fish and cephalopods. It is viviparous and gives birth to one to six young, who are completely self-sufficient. Measures up to 180 centimeters in length and is potentially dangerous.

Nurse shark - *Nebrius ferrugineus*

Shark with a tapered body flattened in the ventral area. The head is slightly pointed and the mouth, facing down, is located beyond the eyes. There are two long lateral barbels on the snout. There are two dorsal fins on the back, close together, with the first one higher and more developed. The tail is quite elongated. Color depends on the age of the individual and its habitat, and varies from gray to brownish. It is nocturnal. By day it is inactive and stays in caves and recesses in the reef. It feeds on fish and cephalopods and can reach over 3 meters in length.

Whitetip Reef Shark - *Triaenodon obesus*

Elongated and fusiform with characteristic white spots on the apex of the first dorsal fin and tip of the caudal lobe, which is rather elongated. The snout is short and wide, and the mouth has small teeth. A territorial species, it is commonly found resting on sandy seabeds or within caverns. It is considered harmless to man, but should not be disturbed. It is more active at night, when it hunts its prey, primarily fish, using its well-developed olfactory sense. It is viviparous and gives birth to one to five young. Measures up to two meters in length.

Hammerhead Shark - *Sphyrna lewini*

The most common type of hammerhead shark. Easily recognizable due to the unique form of the head, wide laterally and flattened at the ends, where the eyes are located. It has a whitish belly and gray-brown dorsal area. The pectoral and dorsal fins are well-developed and have dark spots. In general solitary, it may gather in large groups when it comes to the coast for reproduction. It is viviparous and may give birth to more than 30 young. It feeds primarily on rays, but also fish and squid. Measures over 4 meters in length.

Leopard Shark - *Stegostoma fasciatum*

Massive, fusiform body with characteristic longitudinal ribbing. The pectoral fins are quite developed and the tail is elongated, sometimes as long as the entire body. It is yellow-brown with black spots, while young individuals are brown with yellow bands. The mouth is small, located below the pointed snout and ahead of the eyes. It is nocturnal. During the day it can be seen resting on the bottom of shallow lagoons. It feeds on crustaceans, members of the eel family and more rarely fish. It is ovoviviparous and lays eggs in a violet and black egg case. It can reach over three and a half meters in length.

Giant Manta - *Manta birostris*

Its unmistakable form makes it easily recognizable, with large pectoral fins that may be as much as 5 meters wide. It has two mobile cephalic fins on the head that it uses to direct the plankton on which it feeds into its mouth. The flattened posterior portion ends in a thin tail. The upper part is black, with a white ventral area. It has a few black spots on the belly that can be used to distinguish one individual from another. It can weigh over a ton.

Eagle Ray - *Aetobatus narinari*

Rhomboid-shaped body with very well-developed pectoral fins similar to wings. The back is black with dense white spots, while the belly is white. The very long tail, up to twice as long as the body, has various serrated spines. The head is rather high and ends with a pointed, flat snout. It feeds on mollusks, crustaceans and worms that it finds on the bottom of shallow lagoons. It is ovoviviparous and gives birth to one to four young after a year of gestation.

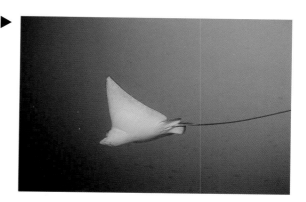

Stingray - *Taeniura melanospilos*

A large ray with a disk that may be over two meters in diameter. The back is dark gray with lighter, irregular spots, while the belly is whitish. The body ends in a robust tail with a stinger. It lives on the sea floor, but is also a good swimmer. It feeds on sand eels, crabs and other crustaceans, which it uncovers from the sand with its pectoral fins. It is ovoviviparous and may give birth to 2 to 7 young.

Bluespotted Ribbontail Stingray - *Taeniura lymma*

The discoid, flattened body is more or less elongated and ends in a compressed tail with two toothed, poisonous stingers. The back is yellow-brown with blue spots, while the belly is white. The mouth, located underneath, has rows of small teeth that it uses to grasp the crustaceans and mollusks on which it feeds, uncovering them with rapid blows of its fin. It lives on sandy seabeds. The disk may reach one meter in diameter, and the tail may be one meter long.

Gray Moray - *Siderea grisea*

A small moray with an elongated, slightly flattened body and pointed snout. It is gray-yellow with distinct small spots on the head that form special patterns. The mouth has small conical teeth on the upper mandible. It is the most common moray of the Red Sea and lives in shallow waters. It's not uncommon to see it swimming outside its den among the protuberances of the reef. It is more active at night, when it hunts small fish. May reach a length of 50 centimeters.

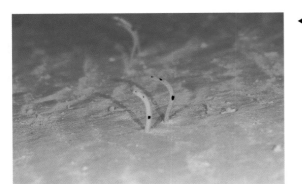

Sand Eel - *Gorgasia sillneri*

Elongated, cylindrical, gray body with a few darker spots. Lives on sandy flat areas in groups of over a thousand individuals. It can be seen protruding out of the sand for almost the entire length of its body in a characteristic question mark position. It feeds on plankton, which it catches by darting forward rapidly. It may measure up to 50 centimeters in length.

Reef Lizardfish - *Synodus variegatus*

The body is tapered and cylindrical, flattened at the belly. The snout is short and pointed and ends in an oblique mouth with pointed teeth facing backward, located on the tongue as well. The eyes are in a frontal position. The color varies from red to brown, with lighter spots on the flanks. Measures up to 20 centimeters.

Squirrelfish - *Sargocentron spiniferum*

High and compressed body covered with large scales. The snout is pointed with an oblique mouth tilted upward, and very large, convex eyes are evidence of its nocturnal habits. The tail is typically forked. It is red, while the edges of the scales are lighter. It is very aggressive and will boldly defend its territory. It feeds on crustaceans and worms. Measures up to 45 centimeters in length.

Red Soldierfish - *Myripristis murdjan*

The body is oval and slightly compressed, with large, sharp scales, and it is bright red with a black spot near the branchial operculum. More active at night, by day it gathers in small groups at the base of the reef or the mouth of small caves. It feeds primarily on zooplankton, but also on shrimp and small fish. Measures up to 30 centimeters in length.

Pipefish - *Corythoichthys schultzi*

Slender, cylindrical, elongated body. The snout is elongated and ends in a mouth similar to a sucking pump, which the pipefish uses to suck up the small crustaceans on which it feeds. The dorsal fin is small, and the caudal fin is fan-shaped. The basic color is olive gray streaked with black. Males have a central sac where females deposit the eggs, which are then fecundated and incubated until they hatch. Measures up to 15 centimeters in length.

Crocodilefish - *Papilloculiceps longiceps*

Fish with a flattened body at the front that tends to taper at the back. The characteristic form of the head, flat with a large mouth facing upwards, have given it its name. The body is scattered with appendages and growths that increase its mimetic abilities. It lives on detrital and sandy floors, where it lies in wait for the small fish on which it feeds. It is gray-brown in color with darker spots. Measures up to 70 centimeters in length.

Cornetfish - *Fistularia commersoni*

The cylindrical body is very elongated. The long, tubular mouth can change shape and is used to suck up prey. The caudal fin is triangular, with a long central filament. The base color is silvery green, but may change to mimic various environments. It often swims near much larger fish to approach its prey unseen. It is active both by day and night. Can reach up to 150 centimeters in length.

Tasseled Scorpionfish - *Scorpaenopsis barbata*

Large scorpaenid with a massive, high body, The head is large, armed with spines, and its mouth faces upward. The entire head has irregular, fleshy appendages. It coloring is extremely mimetic and adapts to the type of sea floor. When disturbed, it becomes red. The rays of the dorsal and branchial spines are poisonous. Because it is so mimetic, it is a potential danger. The species is more active at night. It reaches 30 centimeters in length.

Stonefish - *Synanceia verrucosa*

Stubby, slightly elongated and globular body covered with fleshy ridges and spines. The eyes are on the top of the head and the mouth opens almost vertically to the snout. The pectoral fins have very developed fans and the dorsal fin has robust spines connected to poison sacs. Contact may be fatal. Its coloring is highly mimetic and makes it practically invisible, and it will turn red only if disturbed. A skilled predator, it feeds on fish. It reaches 40 centimeters in length.

Longhorned Lionfish - *Pterois radiata*

Scorpaenid with a robust, high, slightly compressed body. It is reddish brown with white streaks. The rays of the pectoral fins are detached from each other, while those of the dorsal fin are joined by a membrane only at the base: all spines are poisonous. If disturbed, it is potentially dangerous. It has a sturdy, extendible beak at the front of the head that it uses to suck up its prey, which includes small fish and crustaceans. Measures up to 25 centimeters in length.

♂

♀

Lyretail Coralfish - *Pseudanthias squamipinnis*

Tapered, slightly compressed body with a clearly bilobate caudal fin. The dorsal fin, especially in males, has a very pronounced spiny ray. The color varies depending on sex: females are red-orange with violet veining around the eyes, while males are violet-fuchsia with a yellow spot on the flanks. It is gregarious and lives in large schools organized into various harems consisting of one or two males and about ten females. Measures about 15 centimeters in length.

Spotted Grouper - *Plectropomus pessuliferus*

The body is robust, elongated and fusiform, with a prominent snout and slightly concave tail. It is brownish-red, but depending on the situation can change to any shade of red and yellow, with wide vertical bands of darker color. The belly is light and there are irregular blue spots on the entire body, fins included. It is carnivorous. It may reach over 100 centimeters in length.

Yellowedged Grouper - *Variola louti*

Grouper with elongated body and rounded snout. The dorsal and anal fins have an elongated back edge. The tail has a typical crescent shape with elongated lobes. It is reddish with small blue and yellow spots; the edge of the fins is yellow. It is solitary and will defend its territory. It feeds on fish. Measures up to 80 centimeters in length.

Red Coral Grouper - *Cephalopholis miniata*

The body is massive, elongated and slightly compressed. The head is robust and the lower jaw prominent. All fins, including the caudal fin, are rounded at the end. It is a vivid red-orange with blue spots. It lives in harems composed of a male and a variable number of females, who will defend their territory. It feeds on small fish, especially anthias. Measures up to 40 centimeters in length.

Redmouth Grouper - *Aethaloperca rogaa*

Easily recognizable by the very high, compressed body profile. The color varies from brown to black. A peculiar characteristic is the orange color inside the mouth and the opercula. A territorial species, it usually lives near the large schools of glassfish on which it feeds. Measures up to 60 centimeters in length.

Longnose Hawkfish - *Oxycirrithes typus*

The body is very elongated and compressed and ends in a long, pointed snout. The well-developed pectoral fins are used to rest on the branches of gorgonians, which it mimics through the red streaks on its sides in a checkerboard pattern. The dorsal fin is spiny and ends in a series of tufts. It lives in harems where the males are the largest individuals, reaching a length of 13 centimeters.

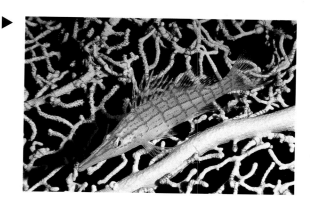

Pixy Hawkfish - *Cirrhitichthys oxycephalus*

The body is fusiform and slightly compressed. The head is pointed and the mouth has rather large lips. The fin running along its entire back have tufts of cirri at the ends. The background color is whitish with irregular red spots. The wide pectoral fins are used to rest on stony corals. It lives in harems of one male and 4 - 5 females. Measures up to 10 centimeters.

Blackside Hawkfish - *Paracirrhites forsteri*

Tapered, high, slightly compressed body. The head is rounded and the snout is short. The spiny rays of the dorsal fin have no barbels; the robust pectoral fins are used as a support. The background color is yellowish, with a dark longitudinal band which is more evident in young individuals. The darker head is speckled with small black spots. It feeds on fish. Can be up to 22 centimeters in length.

Goggle-Eye - *Priacanthus hamrur*

The body is oval, high and compressed. The single dorsal fin extends along almost the entire back, and the tail is forked with elongated lobes. The mouth is large and tilted upward; the wide, protruding eyes reveal its nocturnal habits. It is red but can change rapidly and take on a silvery glint. It feeds on cephalopods and crustaceans. Measures up to 40 centimeters in length.

Orange-Spotted Jack - *Carangoides bajad*

Has a tapered, oval body and a pointed snout ending in a mouth with various rows of teeth. The caudal fin is triangular and deeply incised. It is silvery with small orange spots on the flanks. Depending on the situation, it can rapidly change color and become brilliant orange. It is solitary or swims in small groups in the surface areas of the reef. It can reach 50 centimeters in length.

Bigeye Trevally - *Caranx sexfasciatus*

The body is long and tapered, and the head is rather square. The eyes are large, evidence of its nocturnal habits. The back of the lateral line has horny, raised dentations. The lobes of the tail are at right angles. The color is silvery green, tending to become lighter on the belly. It lives in schools and hunts using attack strategies similar to wolves. Measures up to 85 centimeters in length.

Snubnose Pompano - *Trachinotus blochii*

The oval body is high and compressed, with a rounded head. The caudal fin is quite wide and deeply incised, with black-edged lobes. It is silvery, with golden tones on the snout and around the lips. The edge of the anal fin has yellow tones. As an adult, usually swims in pairs in the near the surface of coral reefs. When young, it prefers shallow, sandy lagoons. Can reach 65 centimeters in length.

Bluefin Trevally - *Caranx melampygus*

Tapered, high and compressed body. The pointed snout ends in a wide mouth armed with a double row of teeth. The falcate caudal fin has very long lobes. The color is silvery blue speckled with small blue spots. The fins are blue except for the pectoral fins, which are yellow. The back part of the lateral line has a series of raised dentations. Swims in small schools and hunts throughout the day, feeding on fish. Measures up to 100 centimeters in length.

Bluestriped Snapper - *Lutjanus kasmira*

The body is elongated and compressed, the snout conical and the mouth has well-defined lips and strong teeth. The anal and dorsal fins are square. The tail is truncated. The basic color is yellow, with a whitish belly. There are four horizontal blue stripes on each flank. The fins are a uniform yellow. It is nocturnal and lives in dense schools. It reaches 35 centimeters in length.

Red Snapper - *Lutjanus bohar*

The robust body is elongated and high. The pointed snout ends in a large mouth armed with sharp teeth. The caudal fin is slightly incised. The color is brown on the back, shading to light red on the belly. The fins are black, It is usually solitary, but during the mating season forms schools of hundreds of individuals. It feeds on fish, gastropods and crabs. More active during the day. Measures 75 centimeters in length.

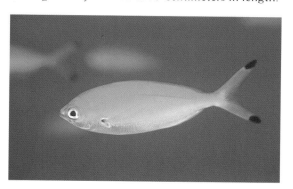

Blackspotted Sweetlips - *Plecthorinchus gaterinus*

The robust, tapered body is slightly compressed. The snout is short and convex. The eyes are large and the mouth has two thick lips. The vivid color is unmistakable, with a light background with numerous black spots that appear on the fins as well, which are yellow. The species is gregarious and inactive during the day. It feeds on small benthic invertebrates. Reaches up to 45 centimeters in length.

Humpback Red Snapper - *Lutjanus gibbus*

Compressed, high body, especially in the central part of the back. The caudal fin has rounded lobes. The background color is brick red, darker on the back. It is gregarious during the day, and more active at night, when it hunts fish and invertebrates. Measures up to 50 centimeters in length.

Spotted Snapper - *Lutjanus monostigma*

Has a tapered, high, slightly compressed body. The pronounced snout has a large mouth with a prominent lower jaw. The tail is slightly concave. The large eyes are evidence of its nocturnal habits. During the day it gathers is shadowy areas. It is silvery yellow. Feeds on fish and crustaceans. It reaches 60 centimeters in length.

Blue Fusilier - *Caesio suevica*

The body is cylindrical and rather elongated. The conical snout ends in a small mouth that can extend out to grasp the particles of plankton on which it feeds. The tail is clearly forked, with a black spot edged in white on the tips. It is silvery blue. It is diurnal and swims in large schools in plankton-rich areas. Measures up to 20 centimeters in length.

Yellowfin Goatfish - *Mulloides vanicolensis*

The body is tapered, with a pointed, high head. The lower jaw has two short barbels. The background color is silvery with a longitudinal yellow stripe that runs from the eye to the tail. It is gregarious and lives in schools of hundreds of individuals. It is more active at night. Measures up to 40 centimeters in length.

Batfish - *Platax orbicularis*

The very high and compressed body gives it a disk-like appearance. The head is slightly elongated and ends in a pointed mouth. The dorsal and anal fins are very rounded and located quite close to the tail. The background color is silvery, with dark gray tones and two vertical bands, one of which crosses the eye. It is omnivorous and gregarious. Measures up to 50 centimeters in diameter.

Blackback Butterflyfish - *Chaetodon melannotus*

The oval body is high and compressed, whitish in color with dense diagonal spots that converge on the back, forming a dark band. The fins are yellow, and a black vertical band can be seen near the eye. The caudal peduncle and bottom edge of the anal fin have a black spot. The snout is short and pointed. It usually lives in pairs among the branches of Acropora corals, on whose polyps it feeds. It can reach 15 centimeters in length.

Yellowsaddle Goatfish - *Parupeneus cyclostomus*

High, tapered, slightly compressed body with protruding mouth and two long barbels on the lower jaw. The caudal fin is clearly bilobate. The basic color is yellow, but it may become blue-violet as well. It feeds on small benthic fish, which it uncovers with its barbels. Measures over 40 centimeters in length.

Glassfish - *Parapriacanthus guentheri*

Small fish with elongated, slightly compressed body. The profile is high at the head and tapered toward the tail. The eye is quite large and convex and the mouth is wide, with many teeth. The front part is silvery, while the rest of the body is almost transparent. It is nocturnal, and by day takes shelter in the more shadowy areas of the reef. It feeds on zooplankton. Measures up to 10 centimeters in length.

Longfin Batfish - *Platax teira*

Discoid, compressed body. The head is round with a small, upturned mouth. The dorsal and anal fins are rounded and elongated to the back. There are conspicuous, long yellow ventral fins and the tail is truncated. It is silvery gray with a lighter belly and two wide vertical dark bands, one crossing the eyes. It has a characteristic black spot below the pectoral fin. Lives in schools. Measures up to 50 centimeters long.

Redtailed Butterflyfish - *Chaetodon paucifasciatus*

The body is high and compressed, with a pointed snout. It is whitish in color, with black, angular streaks on the flanks. There are orange bands across the eyes and the back part of the tail and dorsal fin. The tail and fins are edged in yellow. It lives in pairs or small groups near detrital areas. It feeds on polyps of gorgonians and other corals, small crustaceans and algae. Measures up to 15 centimeters in length.

Threadfin Butterflyfish - *Chaetodon auriga*

Very high, compressed body with a concave area at the eyes. The head ends in a pointed, short snout. A clear vertical black band crosses the ocular area. It is whitish with black streaks that form angles at the front, and the posterior area is yellow. The dorsal fin ends in a posterior filamentous ray. It usually swims in pairs, feeds primarily on invertebrates and measures up to 25 centimeters in length.

Raccoon Butterflyfish - *Chaetodon fasciatus*

Elongated, compressed body with elongated snout. The background color is dark yellow with oblique black bands. The eye is surrounded by a black spot surmounted by a white area. The edges of the dorsal, anal and caudal fins are edged in black. Young individuals have a showy, posterior ocellus. It is mostly solitary. It feeds on coral polyps, hydroids and invertebrates. Measures 22 centimeters in length.

Golden Butterflyfish - *Chaetodon semilarvatus*

Species endemic to the Red Sea, with an almost discoid form and nearly uniform golden yellow color with narrow dark stripes on the flanks. The snout is relatively short with a concave upper profile. The eye is surrounded by a bluish spot that reaches the operculum. The pectoral fins are transparent. It can often be found in schools. It feeds on the polyps of soft and stony corals. Measures 20 centimeters in length.

Austrian Butterflyfish - *Chaetodon austriacus*

The prevalent color is yellow, with blue-black streaks on the flanks. The tail, anal fin and back edge of the dorsal fin are black. The body is oval and compressed with a very short snout; the dorsal fin runs along the entire length of the back and the anal fin is quite developed. The snout has a vertical black band that crosses the ocular area. Its diet consists exclusively of polyps. Reaches 12 centimeters in length.

Bannerfish - *Heniochus diphreutes*

Like other Heniochus, this butterflyfish has a characteristic form due to the fourth spiny ray of the dorsal fin, quite elongated at the back. The body is compressed, whitish, with two vertical black bands. The snout is pointed and rather pronounced. It lives in schools that may include hundreds of individuals. It prefers areas with strong currents, as it feeds on zooplankton. Measures about 18 centimeters in length.

Emperor Angelfish - *Pomacanthus imperator*

Fish with a high, elongated body with slightly flattened snout. Diagonal yellow and bluish streaks on the flanks with a yellow caudal fin. Young individuals are dark blue with light concentric bands. It is territorial and usually solitary. It feeds on algae and sponges. If disturbed, it makes loud sounds. Up to 40 centimeters in length.

Red Sea Bannerfish - *Heniochus intermedius*

The body is high and compressed and ends in a short pointed snout. It is whitish-yellow and its flanks have two conspicuous black bands. The ventral area, anal fin and tail are yellow. The dorsal fin ends in a characteristic, very elongated spiny ray. The eyes are masked by a black streak. This fish is territorial, and usually an Acropora umbrella can be found in the center of its territory. It swims in pairs, but can often be found in dense schools. Measures up to 23 centimeters in length.

Regal Angelfish - *Pygoplites diacanthus*

The body is not as high as other angelfish. The mouth is small and terminal. The background color is yellow-orange with eight vertical bands of white surrounded by blue. The caudal fin is rounded, the soft part of the dorsal fin is blue, while the anal fin is orange and blue. Young individuals, who look similar, have a posterior ocellus. It feeds on sponges and Tunicates. Measures 25 centimeters in length.

Yellowband Angelfish - *Pomacanthus maculosus*

High, compressed body with a convex upper head that ends in a short snout. The posterior edges of the dorsal and anal fins end in a long filament consisting of rays fused together. The caudal fin is rounded and is blue and yellow. Body color is bluish with a large yellow spot on the flanks. Young individuals are dark purple with vertical blue and white bands, and change color when they are 10-15 centimeters long. Measures 50 centimeters in length.

Sergeant Major - *Abudefduf sexfasciatus*

Oval, compressed, robust body. The mouth is at the top of the slightly pointed head. It is silvery gray with yellow tones on the back. There are five vertical black bands on the sides and the belly is white. Lives in dense schools near the reef. Feeds on zooplankton, small invertebrates and benthic algae. Measures up to 15 centimeters in length.

Green Chromis - *Chromis viridis*

The body is oval and compressed, with a convex mouth. The tail has two long, deeply incised lobes. The color is a uniform blue-green and in males only, during the mating season, the dorsal fin becomes yellow and black. Lives in schools near coral branches, where it will take refuge if threatened. It feeds on plankton and measures 8 centimeters in length.

Whitebelly Damselfish - *Amblyglyphidodon leucogaster*

The body is high and compressed with a pointed snout, and the mouth has small teeth. The pectoral and anal fins are elongated to the back and the tail is falcate. The edge of the fins and tail is black. It is green with blue tones on the back and a white belly. Lives in small groups and feeds on zooplankton. Measures up to 13 centimeters in length.

Domino Damselfish - *Dascyllus trimaculatus*

Rounded, high and compressed body. The snout is rounded with a small mouth tilted upward, characteristic of fish who feed on plankton. The color is unmistakable, black or brown with three white spots, one on each side and one on the front. When young, it lives associated with anemones, which it abandons as an adult. Forms small harems. Measures up to 14 centimeters in length.

Bigmouth Wrasse - *Epibulus insidiator*

Robust, compressed and elongated body. The head is high and concave at the eyes. The mouth is large and can be extended, resembling a tube. The rays of the anal and dorsal fins are very elongated to the back. The tail is slightly falcate. There is a clear difference in color between the two sexes: the female is completely yellow with a black ray pattern around the eyes, while males have a brown body with a red spot on the back and a white head. It feeds on crabs, shrimp and small fish. Measures up to 35 centimeters in length.

Yellow Damselfish - *Amblyglyphidodon flavilatus*

The body is oval, high and compressed. The head is pointed, with a small mouth armed with teeth. The central fins and clearly triangular tail are rather well-developed. The dominant color is yellow, with white tones on the belly. Feeds on zooplankton, which it captures in rapid darts. Solitary. May reach 10 centimeters in length.

Sulfur Damselfish - *Pomacentrus sulfureus*

The body is slightly oval and compressed. The short, pointed snout ends in a small mouth armed with teeth. The dorsal fin runs along the entire body and becomes symmetrical with the anal fin. The brilliant yellow color tends to become darker on the back. There are clearly visible characteristic black spots at the base of the pectoral fin. It is solitary. Measures 11 centimeters in length.

Cleaner Wrasse - *Labroides dimidiatus*

The body is compressed and cylindrical. The head is pointed and the snout has a mouth full of teeth. It is white-blue with a clear longitudinal black stripe that runs from the mouth, widening to cover the entire tail. It occupies a territory that it transforms into a cleaning station visited by large fish who want to be freed of parasites. Reaches 10 centimeters in length.

Humphead Wrasse - *Cheilinus undulatus*

The largest known wrasse has a high, stubby body. The head is robust, and in adults has a large protuberance on the front. The large mouth has thick lips and can be extended out to suck up its prey. The caudal fin is convex and the uneven fins are elongated to the back. It feeds on crustaceans, urchins and starfish. It is a territorial, solitary species. May reach over 2 meters in length.

Cheeklined Wrasse - *Oxycheilinus digrammus*

Elongated, tapered body with pointed head. The mouth is large and diagonal, tilted upward. The tail is high and truncated. It is reddish brown with a green head with yellow-orange stripes. It feeds on small fish and invertebrates. Measures up to 30 centimeters in length.

Clown Wrasse - *Coris aygula*

High, tapered and slightly compressed body. Males have a frontal protuberance. The tail has characteristic fringes. The species constantly changes color depending on age and sex. Adult males are dark green with blue tones and have a wide, light, vertical band in the mid-section. May reach over 70 centimeters in length.

Klunzinger's Wrasse - *Thalassoma klunzingeri*

Species endemic to the Red Sea. Has a tapered body with slightly pointed head. Two robust canines protrude from the small mouth. The deeply falcate tail has elongated lobes. The base color is greenish with a red horizontal band and some vertical red stripes on the back. The head has concentric red stripes. Measures up to 20 centimeters in length.

Bicolor Parrotfish - *Cetoscarus bicolor*

The robust body is oval and slightly compressed at the sides. The round mouth ends in a sturdy, horny beak. The tail is crescent-shaped with long filaments. Males are brightly colored, green with fuchsia-edged scales. There are numerous fuchsia stripes around the mouth and eyes. The area below the throat is white and the caudal fin is fuchsia. Females are brown with a wide yellow band along the back. It is territorial and lives in harems. It reaches 90 centimeters in length.

African Wrasse - *Coris africana*

The body is cylindrical, tapered and slightly compressed. The head is conical with a small mouth with teeth. The first few rays of the dorsal fin are quite high on the back in adults. The color is dark red with narrow greenish veining. The head has green and red streaks. A vertical green band appears just behind the branchial operculum in males. Reaches 40 centimeters in length.

Longnose Parrotfish - *Hipposcarus harid*

Tapered body with pointed head ending in a conical snout. The lower jaw is narrower and shorter than the upper one. The tail is falcate with threadlike lobes. In females, the color is blue-green with lilac tones on the back and snout. Males are greenish with irregular brown spots on the head and flanks. It lives in groups of mainly females. Measures 55 centimeters in length.

Rusty Parrotfish - *Scarus ferrugineus*

Tapered, oval body with round snout and conspicuous dental plates. The caudal fin is truncated with slightly pointed lobes. Males are green on the back and bluish on the belly. Lives in territorial harems with one dominant male and numerous females, which are brown with yellowish vertical bands and a yellow tail. May reach 40 centimeters in length.

Bullethead Parrotfish - *Scarus sordidus*

Tapered, regular body with head rounded at the end. The lips reveal the dental plates it uses to scrape the surface of stony corals to remove the algae covering them. The tail is truncated. Males are green with a wide lighter band on the caudal peduncle. The edges of the scales are pink. The snout has several blue stripes. It is the most common fish of the Red Sea. Measures 40 centimeters in length.

♂

Bumphead Parrotfish - *Scarus gibbus*

Fish with high, oval, robust body. The profile of the head is almost vertical, and the dental plates are quite conspicuous. The crescent-shaped tail has elongated lobes. Males are green with reddish tones, while females are yellowish near the dorsal area and brown on the belly. The area under the throat is blue. Like all parrotfish, it grinds stony corals to feed on the algae and is diurnal. At night, it wraps itself in a cocoon of mucus it secretes from its mouth to protect itself from predators. Measures 70 centimeters in length.

♀

Barracuda - *Sphyraena barracuda*

The body is very elongated and cylindrical. The head is long and conical and ends in a mouth with powerful teeth and a jutting lower jaw. The back is square with two separate dorsal fins; the caudal fin is deeply incised. The background color is silvery with greenish reflections on the back, with a lighter ventral area. There are dark vertical stripes on the flanks. It swims slowly and is solitary, and it is not uncommon to see it near the surface, lying in wait. It may reach up to two meters in length.

Orange-Spotted Goby - *Valencennea puellaris*

The body is elongated. The front portion is cylindrical and compressed in the caudal region. The belly is flat. The head is large with eyes in a dorsal position. The large pectoral fins are used as a support and for moving short distances on the floor. It is whitish with yellow-orange stripes on the flanks. Lives in pairs on sandy floors, where it uses its mouth to dig a tunnel-like den. Measures up to 15 centimeters in length.

Lemon Goby - *Gobiodon citrinus*

The body is elongated and slightly compressed. The rounded head has a frontal, slightly protruding mouth. The caudal fin is convex and almost round. The dorsal fins are rounded and rather high, and the well-developed pectoral fins are used as a support. The color makes this goby unmistakable: it is brilliant yellow on the belly and head. Lives in small groups among Acropora coral branches. Measures up to 7 centimeters in length.

Scissortail Goby - *Ptereleotris evides*

Elongated, slightly compressed body. The head is somewhat pointed with a mouth tilted upward. The caudal fin is highly incised, the first dorsal fin high and rounded, usually kept folded. The almost symmetrical second dorsal fin and the anal fin give it the form of a dart. The color is blue-gray near the front and dark blue to the tail, which is light blue. Lives in pairs on detrital sea floors near its den, where it will rapidly take refuge if threatened. Measures up to 15 centimeters in length.

Steinitz's Goby - *Amblyeleotris steinitzi*

Elongated, slightly compressed body. The head has globular eyes in a dorsal position and the mouth tilted upward, with large lips. The caudal fin is broad and rounded, the dorsal fins quite distinct and the pectoral fins well-developed to act as a support on the sea floor. It is light-colored with five vertical brown bands on the flanks. Lives on sandy seabeds in a den it shares with a shrimp from the genus Alpheus. Can measure up to 8 centimeters in length.

Red Sea Blenny - *Ecsenius dentex*

Elongated, compressed body tapering toward the tail, with a square head. The mouth, which opens on the lower part of the head, is armed with numerous teeth. The eyes are large. The caudal fin is truncated. It is whitish with longitudinal black hatching. A black line runs from the lower jaw to the operculum. Measures up to 8 centimeters in length.

Midas Blenny - *Ecsenius midas*

Elongated, slightly compressed body, higher at the head, with the mouth in the lower part of the head. The dorsal fin runs along the entire body, and the robust pectoral fins are used to rest on the reef. The color may vary from orange brown to yellow. Some individuals may be blue. It feeds on zooplankton, which it catches by darting rapidly into the column of water. Measures up to 13 centimeters in length.

Desjardin's Tang - *Zebrasoma desjardinii*

The high, compressed discoid body ends in a pointed snout and small mouth. The dorsal and anal fins are well-developed and have a rounded profile. The tail has a slightly convex edge. The color is grayish-brown with light vertical stripes. The head and tail are speckled with white. It generally lives in pairs, feeding on algae. Reaches 40 centimeters in length.

Yellowtail Tang - *Zebrasoma xanthurum*

The discoid body is high and compressed, with an elongated snout that ends in a small mouth equipped with horny plates. The dorsal and anal fins are well-developed, rounded and almost symmetrical. The color is blue with small dark spots on the head, while the pectoral fins and tail are yellow. Measures up to 25 centimeters in length.

Lipstick Tang - *Naso lituratus*

Compressed oval body, high near the front. The pointed snout has an angular profile. The crescent-shaped caudal fin has lobes that end in long filaments. Each side of the caudal peduncle has two spines curving forward. The color is brown with a yellow spot in front; the fins are edged in yellow. It feeds on brown algae. Reaches 40 centimeters in length.

Unicorn Tang - *Naso hexacanthus*

Tapered body with oval profile. The snout ends in a point with a small mouth armed with numerous teeth. The caudal peduncle has robust spines and the fin has a truncated tip. The dorsal and anal fins, which run along the body's profile, are usually folded. The color varies from brown to green, and during courting males take on a light blue color. Measures up to 70 centimeters in length.

Unicornfish - *Naso unicornis*

The body is tapered, robust and slightly compressed. The head is high and ends in a pointed snout. A peculiar characteristic of large adults is a protuberance similar to a horn before the eyes. The caudal peduncle has two robust spines pointed forward. The color is olive and the fins are edged in blue. It feeds on brown algae. Measures up to 70 centimeters.

Kole Tang - *Ctenochaetus striatus*

The body with its oval and compressed profile ends in a snout with very enlarged lips. The caudal fin is falcate. The color is brownish-olive with narrow light stripes; the pectoral fins have shades of yellow. It lives in schools and feeds on green encrusting algae. This characteristic makes it one of the few herbivores that occasionally have "ciguattera" toxins in its flesh. Measures about 26 centimeters in length.

Undulate Triggerfish - *Balistapus undulatus*

The body is oval, high and rather compressed. The head is quite developed and the mouth is small, with robust, chisel-shaped teeth. The first dorsal fin is triangular, with the first ray spiny and large. The dorsal and anal fins are the same height. The caudal peduncle has several spines pointing forward. It is greenish with orange stripes. It feeds on sea urchins, crustaceans and small fish. Measures up to 30 centimeters in length.

Titan Triggerfish - *Balistoides viridescens*

The body is robust and oval, characteristic of the family. The head is large with a furrow between the eyes. The mouth has strong teeth. The color is olive, with the scales edged in yellow. It feeds primarily on urchins and starfish. A very territorial species, it becomes aggressive during the mating period and will not hesitate to attack even divers. It can reach up to 75 centimeters in length.

Sohal Surgeonfish - *Acanthurus sohal*

Rather compressed oval body. The head is rounded, with a high profile. The caudal fin is quite falcate with elongated lobes. The horny blades at the sides of the peduncle are extremely sharp and brilliant orange. It is bluish with narrow black longitudinal streaks. The belly is whitish. It is an excellent swimmer and will defend its territory from other herbivore fish. Measures up to 40 centimeters in length. .

Stellate Rabbitfish - *Siganus stellatus*

The body is oval and compressed, the small, pointed mouth armed with teeth, with a slight furrow at eye height. The dorsal fin runs from the head to the tail, and is preceded by a spiny ray connected to poison sacs. The tail is triangular and deeply incised. The color is grayish with dense black spots. Usually lives in pairs and seeks out the algae on which it feeds. Measures up to 40 centimeters in length.

Redtooth Triggerfish - *Odonus niger*

The body is high and compressed, with the mouth turned upward and bright red, exposed teeth in the upper jaw. The dorsal and anal fins are well-developed and symmetrical. The deeply falcate tail has very elongated lobes. It is bluish with violet reflections. It feeds on zooplankton. It measures about 40 centimeters in length.

Scrawled Filefish - *Aluterus scriptus*

Tapered, very elongated, compressed body. The long snout, concave in the upper portion, ends in a small mouth turned upward. The caudal fin is long and ample and is usually folded. It is grayish with blue and black spots and stripes. It feeds on hydroids and algae and is solitary. It may reach 100 centimeters in length.

Boxfish - *Ostracion cubicus*

Robust, square body that looks like a box. In adult fish, the stubby snout has a protuberance. The anal fins are located near the caudal peduncle. The caudal fin acts as a rudder and is used only in case of flight. It feeds on algae and invertebrates. Although it is protected by sturdy armor, when it senses danger it defends itself by secreting a toxic substance. May reach 40 centimeters in length.

Masked Puffer - *Arothron diadematosus*

Oval body with rounded snout that ends in a mouth with large lips. The teeth are found in plates, of which there are two for each jaw. The dorsal and anal fins are positioned to the rear, and the caudal fin has a palette shape. It is light-colored with dark bands around the eyes and mouth. The skin has no scales. Measures up to 30 centimeters in length.

Harlequin Filefish - *Oxymonacanthus halli*

Oval, compressed body ending in a pointed snout. The orange, tubular mouth is small and turned upwards. It is green with small orange spots all over the body. There is a long dorsal spine over the eye. Lives in small groups among the branches of Acropora corals, on whose polyps it feeds. Measures 10 centimeters in length.

Sharpnose Puffer - *Canthigaster valentini*

This puffer has a slightly compressed body and head and is dotted with small spines that can be seen only when it puffs up. The snout is elongated and the mouth is protractile. It is yellowish in color, with conspicuous dark spots on the back. There are blue streaks around the eyes and snout. The caudal fin is truncated. Measures about 10 centimeters in length.

Pygmy Puffer - *Canthigaster pygmaea*

The body is elongated, larger in the center, with a pointed snout. The ventral fins are absent, while the dorsal and central fins are to the rear and the caudal fin is rounded. It is brownish with blue spots on the body and blue streaks on the head. If disturbed, it can secrete a toxic substance. It reaches 5-6 centimeters in length.

Porcupinefish - *Diodon hystrix*

The cylindrical body is slightly flattened longitudinally. The mouth has a single dental plate for each jaw. The eyes are quite large, as the fish is nocturnal. There are distinct spines over its entire body, which are raised when the fish swells up to defend itself. It is brownish yellow with dark spots on the back and flanks. It measures about 90 centimeters in length.

Cleaner Shrimp - *Stenopus hispidus*

Very common shrimp with unmistakable series of long white antennae, which it moves to call fish to be cleaned. Its color is almost unmistakable, with white and red stripes. The claws are quite elongated. It feeds on other crustaceans and worms and supplements its diet with parasites that it removes from the skin of the fish it cleans. Lives in pairs, and males have the curious habit of bringing food to the female. Reaches 10 centimeters in length.

Porcelain Crab - *Neopetrolisthes ohshimai*

Small crab whose carapace has regular edges. The three pairs of legs have robust hooks with equal sized claws. Under the head and around the mouth is a series of very mobile claws used to bring food to the mouth. The eyes are close-set with short ocular peduncles. It is yellowish with regular red spots. Lives associated with anemones. Reaches about 3 centimeters in size.

Star Puffer - *Arothron stellatus*

The body is oval, rounded in front and slightly compressed to the back. It swims primarily using the caudal and anal fins. It is light-colored with dark spots all over the body, including the fins. It is the largest of the puffers and feeds on sponges. It is solitary and gathers in groups only during the reproductive period. It may reach one meter in length.

Red Hermit Crab - *Dardanus tinctor*

Large crustacean with body covered in bristles and no rigid carapace. It must live in the empty shell of a conch, which it carries with it like a house, to protect its defenseless body. Normally the claws are different sizes, and like the rest of the feet, are covered in fine hairs. The color varies from red to yellow. The ocular peduncles have yellow and black stripes and black eyes at the tips. Measures up to 10 centimeters in length.

Red Crab - *Carpilius convexus*

Large crustacean with oval shell wider than it is long. The carapace appears convex and has no dentations, like the lower edge. The eyes are well protected by rigid ocular peduncles. One claw is larger than the other. The color is reddish, with yellow streaks on the back. It is nocturnal and feeds on mollusks and dead animals. May reach 20 centimeters in length.

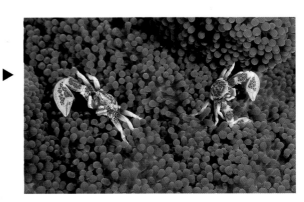

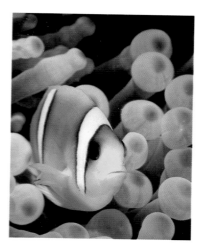

Nudibranch - *Chromodoris quadricolor*

Elongated, thin nudibranch with rather wide mantle. The upper front portion has two plate rhinophores. The posterior section of the back has a prominent branchial tuft with tentacles similar to feathers that retract rapidly if the animal senses danger. The edge of the mantle is yellow, and inside there are alternating circles of white, black and blue. It can be seen crawling on the red sponges on which it feeds. Reaches about 5 centimeters in size.

Sea Cucumber - *Thelenota ananas*

The cylindrical, elongated body is covered with skin reinforced by plates and calcareous spicules. The mouth is at one end of the body and can be extended out, while the anal siphon is at the other end. Lives in contact with the floor, where it swallows detritus that it then ejects after keeping the organic substances. It is unfortunately suffering a rapid decline due to indiscriminate fishing for food use, especially in the Asian market. Up to 75 centimeters long.

Clownfish - *Amphiprion bicinctus*

Oval, rounded, slightly compressed body. The head is convex with mouth turned upward and large lips. It has numerous teeth. It is yellow-orange shading to dark on the back and head. The flanks have two vertical white-blue bands edged in black. It lives associated with various types of anemones in family units made up of a dominant female and several smaller males. Highly territorial, it will drive any possible competitors from its anemone. Measures about 12 centimeters in length

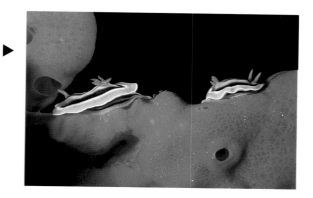

Nudibranch - *Nembrotha megalocera*

Nudibranch endemic to the Red Sea, with a cylindrical, elongated body with robust foot. There are two plate rhinophores on the head with a rigid support at the base. There is a branchial tuft about halfway up the body, with tentacles that can be retracted into the special pocket. The color shades from a white belly to a black back. The tail, branchial tuft and rhinophores are red. The frontal appendages and edge of the foot are violet. It reaches 10 centimeters in length.

Wreathy-Tuft Tube Worm - *Sabellastarte sanctijosephi*

Sedentary worm that sinks its tube, made of mucus and mud, into sandy sea floors. The showy branchial tuft is composed of feathery tentacles that may be one color or variegated. It is very sensitive to variations in light or water pressure, and quickly retreats into the tube, which has no closing operculum. It feeds on plankton, which it captures through the dense network formed by the plumes of its tentacles.

Crown-of-Thorns Starfish - *Acanthaster planci*

Large starfish that can be recognized by its large arms, up to twenty-two of them, armed with robust spines that are also found on the upper part of the disk. It is sadly famous for being a species that destroys corals. It wraps its stomach around stony corals and extrudes it to eat the coral polyps. Its spines are covered with a toxic mucus that causes very painful stings. It is more active at night. Reaches 40 centimeters in diameter.

Chickenfoot Sponge - *Clathria reinwardti*

Branching sponge that forms intricate colonies of soft red bushes. The tissue is covered with dense pores that suck up water carrying in nutritive substances and oxygen. Lives in symbiosis with a special type of algae, which gives it its bright carmine red color.

Crinoid - *Comanthina nobilis*

Echinoderm that is easily recognizable by the numerous tentacles similar to feathery arms, which vary in number from five to two hundred. The pinnules located on the arms have the task of capturing plankton and conveying it to the mouth, located on the upper portion of the disk. Underneath, there are numerous appendages used to anchor to the substratum or move quickly on the sea floor. It is more active at night, and by day can easily be spotted rolled up in a ball.

Organ Pipe Sponge - *Siphonochalina siphonella*

Sponge with a characteristic elongated, tubular cylindrical form. Can be found in colonies where various pipes run from the same base. It is a filter feeder equipped with pores through which water enters, from which it withdraws oxygen and microscopic food particles. Its rigid form is due to the silica ribbing held together by a substance known as spongin.

Leather Coral - *Sarcophyton trocheliophorum*

This coral forms colonies firmly anchored to the floor by a sturdy peduncle with no polyps. The lobed upper portion is scattered with tufts of retracting polyps that have eight feathery tentacles. It may occupy wide portions of reef, inhibiting the growth of other corals by secreting a toxin. The color is greenish yellow when the polyps are closed, and becomes very light when opened.

Anemone - *Heteractis magnifica*

Large actinia with characteristic tentacles up to 10 centimeters long, cylindrical with a rounded, greenish brown tip. The tentacles are stinging and associated with zooxanthellae algae, which determine its color. For this reason, it prefers well-illuminated surface waters. There is a pedal disk under the mantle that it uses to adhere to the substratum. A peculiar characteristic is the ability of the lower side of the bright red mantle to contract. Lives in symbiosis with clownfish.

Gorgonian - *Subergorgia hicksoni*

The species forms large, thickly branched fans fused together to create very large structures. The colonies are formed by large branches solidly fixed to the floor, from which run smaller branches that form the fans that are so admired in these corals. The skeleton is horny, and the polyps have eight feathery tentacles that create the difference in color, depending on whether they are open or closed. They feed on plankton carried in by the current, so that they are more numerous where there is more water movement. The fans can reach up to 2 meters in size.

Alcyonarian - *Dendronephthya*

More commonly known as soft coral, Dendronephthya is perhaps the best known representative of this group. A colonial anthozoan, it builds typically arborescent structures with a wealth of branches. There is a conspicuous rubbery supporting trunk rendered rigid by calcareous endings. The polyps have eight feathery tentacles it uses to capture the plankton on which it feeds. The color of these soft corals varies greatly, running from white to red and from red to violet. The dimensions are quite variable, depending on the coral's state of activity.

Pipe Organ Coral - *Tubipora musica*

Forms extensive colonies with polyps that look like a blooming flower bed when opened. The polyps are almost always expanded and pulse continuously to oxygenate the colony and thus the algae that provide nourishment. The skeleton consist of calcareous tubes within which the polyps retract when they feel threatened.

Umbrella Coral - *Acropora hyacinthus*

The Acropora family is certainly the most common of Red Sea stony corals, with over fifteen species. It builds various types of structures. In this case, the branches are short and very dense, forming a sort of umbrella. The color is generally grayish, and they may become up to 2 meters in diameter and one meter high.

Fire Coral - *Millepora dichotoma*

Belongs to the class of Hydrozoa and has a calcareous skeleton like that of stony corals. Has short yellowish branches with ivory-colored tips. Narrow, filiform, highly stinging polyps extend from the pores of the calcareous structure. Millepora is very common in surface waters, as it is highly dependent on symbiotic algae that provide it with nutrients.

Brain Coral - *Favia favus*

The colonies of these polyps form massive structures and are positioned in a way that makes them look like an enormous honeycomb. It completely colonizes large, isolated rocky formations, inhibiting the growth of other corals by emitting a poisonous substance. It is usually green brown.
The polyps expand only at night and are extremely sensitive to changes in light.

Staghorn Coral - *Acropora nobilis*

Very branched colony with long shoots that look like antlers. It may colonize vast areas of the reef, forming calcareous tangles that offer shelter to numerous species of fish. Acropora nobilis is more frequent near the surface of the reef, due to light and water movement. It is one of the most delicate of the Acropora genus, due to the length of its branches.

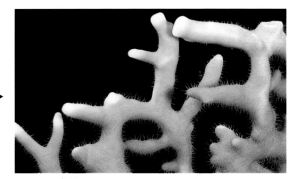

Raspberry Coral - *Pocillopora verrucosa*

Stony coral formation with short branches whose polyps are most expanded at night. The polyps form little clusters that look like bunches of raspberries. The purple color is typical of colonies that live at shallow depths and make the most use of sunlight. Numerous species of crabs find shelter among its branches.

Hump Coral - *Porites lutea*

Imposing stony coral formations with a globular form that usually colonizes slopes of the reef in a form that resembles a hood. The surface has no significant protuberances, but appears rather smooth. It prefers surface areas of the reef and grows less than one centimeter a year. It is yellowish in color, brighter on the upper portion.

Colonial Anemone - *Amphianthus sp.*

Small actinia that forms colonies on supports well-exposed to the current. Common on skeleton branches of dead gorgonians. The pedal disk adheres perfectly even to small surfaces and can be superimposed on others. The tentacles are in concentric rows around the oral disk, where the mouth opening is clearly visible. Lives associated with symbiotic algae that prefer well-lighted waters with currents. The tentacles are milky white, like the disk, which is also variegated with brown.

Lettuce Coral - *Turbinaria mesenterina*

The contorted form of this coral makes it look like a head of lettuce. The volutes of the laminae look curled up like dry, yellowish green leaves. Most of the polyps are concentrated on the top edges of the laminae. Colonies in shallow water look more curled up and contorted. Larger ones may be over two meters in diameter.

Sun or Orange Cup Coral - *Tubastrea aurea*

Arborescent stony coral colony with characteristic golden yellow color of the tentacles. The corallites have an elongated tubular form, and at the tips are long tentacles with cilia around the mouth apparatus. It prefers shadowy areas, as it is totally lacking zooxanthellae.

Christmas Tree Worm - *Spirobranchus giganteus*

This curious worm has a characteristic fir tree shape and lives a sedentary life in its tube affixed to stony coral carbonate. The visible portion consists of two spiral-shaped branchial tufts in variegated colors. It is sensitive to environmental changes, and in case of danger will retract into its tube, which closes with a strong operculum. It feeds on plankton. Measures 3 centimeters in height.

Giant Clam - *Tridacna gigas*

Large, colorful bivalve mollusk with undulating valves from which the dorsal portion of the mollusk protrudes. When the valves are open, two apertures can be seen, which connect the siphons with the alimentary and respiratory apparatuses. The color of the mantle varies depending on the concentration of zooxanthellae. It has sensory organs sensitive to changes in light, which control valve closure. It is considered the largest bivalve in the world, and can reach a length of 130 centimeters.

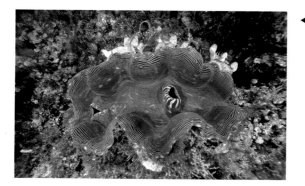

All the photographs in this guide were provided by Claudio Cangini except the following:
Antonio Attini / Archvio White Star: page 16A.
Stefano Bausani: pages 6D, 9E, 48D, 53C, 65A, 70C, 71F, 81F, 94A, 95D, 106A, 107E.

ACKNOWLEDGEMENTS

The authors would like to thank:
- NASE (National Academy of Scuba Educators) for their advice on the Equipment section.
- Valerio, Filippo and Giuseppe from the TGI Diving Center in El-Gouna for their helpfulness, professionalism and friendliness.
- Walter, Massimo, Alessandro and the whole staff of DIVE IN in Hurghada for their assistance and detailed knowledge of the diving areas.
- Clara Tenderini of Kuoni-Gastaldi for her interest and the logistical handling of the expedition to Egypt.
- The staff and management of the ARABIA Beach Hotel in Hurghada for their hospitality and service.
- Luciano and Loredana of ORIGINAL TOUR, tour operator of Rome, for their technical assistance.

Last but not least, we would like to thank our dear friend, Benito "Benny" Augurelli, the volcanic owner of FREE SHARK, for the technical material and equipment. Also Fabio, Luigi, Gianluca and everyone at SUB & SEA for their usual helpfulness and professionalism.

And thanks for the patience of all the fish in the Red Sea
who posed for us.